Bear with Me, Amma

Bear with Me, Amma

Memoirs *of*
M.T. VASUDEVAN NAIR
KERALA JYOTHI 2023

Translated by
Gita Krishnankutty

PENGUIN

An imprint of Penguin Random House

HAMISH HAMILTON

USA | Canada | UK | Ireland | Australia
New Zealand | India | South Africa | China | Singapore

Hamish Hamilton is part of the Penguin Random House group of companies
whose addresses can be found at global.penguinrandomhouse.com

Published by Penguin Random House India Pvt. Ltd
4th Floor, Capital Tower 1, MG Road,
Gurugram 122 002, Haryana, India

First published as *Bear with Me, Mother: Memoirs and Stories* by
Viva Books Pvt. Ltd 2010
This revised edition published in Hamish Hamilton by Penguin Random House
India 2023

ISBN 9780670097906

Typeset in Sabon by Manipal Technologies Limited, Manipal
Printed at Replika Press Pvt. Ltd, India

www.penguin.co.in

This is a legitimate digitally printed version of the book and therefore might not
have certain extra finishing on the cover.

To M.T. Ammalu Amma, my mother (1903–53)

She never knew what her youngest son kept scribbling all day during vacations, in the room upstairs in our *pathayappura,* the outhouse. All that bothered her was that the kerosene lamp burned too late into the night—kerosene was a scarce commodity. I had a few stories published while she was still alive.

Again, she knew nothing about them.

She is very much present in most of the memoirs and appears directly in some of the stories in this collection. And her presence can be perceived in the background of the rest.

It was she who narrated to me the youthful marital adventures of the old grandmother in the short story 'Vision'. As children, we were frightened of Velayudhettan (Soul of Darkness), who was put in chains in the woodshed of the house next door to ours. His family was closely related to us. Everyone said he was insane. One evening, there was some commotion outside and people kept shouting that Velayudhan (we called him Velayudhettan since he was older than us) had broken his chains and escaped. I was five or six years old at the time. I saw him walk towards our house, dragging the chains by his feet. Amma came to the portico. Velayudhettan smiled when he saw her and asked for some rice to eat. Amma asked him to sit down on the veranda and served him a meal. He ate well and walked away calmly.

She did not live to see her youngest son make a career in writing. He picked up many of the characters and events that feature in his work from the *endless* stories she used to narrate to her post-dinner audience of women from the neighbourhood and stored them secretly in his mind for future use.

This book is for you, Amma. Bear with me.

Contents

SECTION II: STORIES

Kinship Terms

Achamma   grandmother (father's mother)

Achan   father

Aliyan   brother-in-law

Ammayi   aunt

Aniyathi   younger sister

Cheriamma   aunt (mother's younger sister)

Edathi   elder sister*

Ettan   elder brother

Muthassi   grandmother (mother's mother/
                 father's mother)

Oppa   elder brother

Oppu, Oppol   elder sister

Valiamma   aunt (mother's elder sister)

---

* 'Oppol' and 'Edathi' both mean elder sister. They are used in different regions of Kerala.

The Malayalam Months

Chingam	August–September
Kanni	September–October
Thulam	October–November
Vrischikam	November–December
Dhanu	December–January
Makaram	January–February
Kumbham	February–March
Meenam	March–April
Medam	April–May
Edavam	May–June
Mithunam	June–July
Karkitakam	July–August

SECTION I

MEMOIRS

1

A Moment of Truth

My friends remind me that it is many years since I started on my journey. The body that often labours hard to keep pace with the swiftness of the mind murmurs the same thing to me. People ask: 'Aren't you going to have a celebration?' Of course not. Is not ageing a law of nature just as the change of seasons is? What is there to celebrate?

I do not celebrate my birthdays. For some time now, I have been going to the Mookambika Temple if I can, either on my birthday or on my daughter Ashwathy's, three days later. We eat our meals in Govinda Adigal's house. The temple and its surroundings bring me a sense of infinite peace. Since this decision is not one my family has imposed on me, it makes me happy if am able to go there at least once a year.

I suddenly realize the childhood that seemingly came to an end just yesterday is actually quite distant. The days when I wandered along the slopes of the Tanni hill behind my house, thinking up stories and poems—a pastime a child with no companions could delight in—letting words tumble over one another in his mind and creating a shape, an order for them.

And so, I manage to scrawl something or the other on a piece of paper every day. After a while, these bits of paper start out on a journey, like paper boats being set afloat on the streams of rainwater that gush down from the eaves. They are directed to every publishing house for which I have an address. Many capsize and sink on the way. But the delight in writing persists. And fortunately, some of them are washed ashore and land on the banks of the printers' world. I have, over time, become convinced that this is no child's play.

Writing comes easily in one's twenties and thirties, the period of youth. It is a kind of frenzy, a madness. As soon as I realize that the story I have been carrying around in my mind has taken shape, I want to put it down on paper. I finish my daily work, eat an early dinner in a small restaurant and arrive at the place where I am staying. I do not bother about time. Sometimes it is three in the morning when I finish the first draft. I sleep for a few hours, before gearing up to work again. The words and lines I wrote the day before are still fresh in my mind. The next free day, Sunday, is far away. I need a whole day to make a fair copy. Every night, I note down a few instructions to myself on the margins of the pages I have written. I score out some lines, make changes in others. On Sunday, once I have copied out everything carefully, I can walk out and rejoice. As requests come for stories to publish in special issues of magazines, there are occasions when I have to finish two stories in three weeks and work overtime to meet my deadlines.

In the forties, writing becomes more difficult. The problem is time. I start to write, then find that I must abandon what I have written because I feel it does not sound quite right. Much later, I take up something I had put aside earlier. In this way, I continually write, stop writing and abandon what I wrote. The days go by until suddenly, in a split second, I realize the piece has come out right. I experience a moment of relief and a flood of happiness I can no longer contain within me.

The years keep rolling by. Each of the pieces I wanted to write has taken its place in its appropriate niche in my mind. I discover all kinds of reasons to put off writing at once and hasten to tell myself that I will find time later. If it is summer, I curse the weather. Let this terrible heat abate. Let it rain, let the atmosphere cool down. And when the rains arrive? Wait, don't be in such a hurry. This rain, which makes me feel cold, should not I indulge in the sense of idleness it brings? Cloudy skies, rain falling in sheets. Let it clear out. When nature grows calm again . . .

When I am aware that everything is just right, I am busy. There are too many people around. All right then, let me sit down alone somewhere and go on with my work. A place where there are no people, nothing to disturb me. I find this place, then realize that I need the crowds and the commotion to be just beyond the spot where I am but located in such a way that they do not invade me. The island of solitude I am in intimidates me.

It has been many years since I started to write. But even now, when I sit down to write, I experience the anxiety, the fear of a student seated in front of an answer sheet in the examination hall. When I was young, writing was sheer delight. Now, it is a conflict. An agonized prayer, an invocation, that words may take the precise shape I have in my mind. In the distance, I see, vaguely and unclearly, the instant of happiness when I will sense that everything has fallen into place, and I go on with my desperate efforts to reach it. My heart whispers, it is not that far away, not really. It is the faltering footsteps I take towards that instant that give meaning to life.

2

Bear with Me, Amma

I have spoken on three occasions at functions commemorating the celebrated Malayalam writer Lalithambika Antharjanam. The third occasion was at Thiruvananthapuram, on 24 May 2003, just after I accepted the award instituted in her name.

Rather unexpectedly one day, I received a letter from Antharjanam soon after a few of my stories had been published. The letter began: 'My dear son, stories that are written in the worship of sorrow often fascinate those who are just beginning to write. Sorrow is one of the truths of life. But is it necessary to worship it?'

Amma knew that I was a close friend of her son Mohanan. Which is why she wrote me such a long and affectionate letter, congratulating me but gently rebuking me as well.

I lost many letters that I had wanted to keep. Including this one that began: 'My dear son . . .'—a letter I consider I was singularly fortunate to receive.

I spoke of this letter at two conferences. But I am compelled to speak of it again now.

This time, however, I will start with Amma, my own mother. The reason being that when Vaishakh, my nephew Mohan Babu's son, came to see me this morning, he brought me a photograph of my mother and me. I had seen it somewhere long ago and had thought it was lost. Vaishakh had searched for it, found it and had a new print made.

While speaking about Antharjanam's letter, I realized that Amma had never written me a letter! Although she knew how to read and write, she never wrote letters. It was I who wrote them for her when she found it necessary. She would sit down on the floor, stretch out her legs, ponder over the sentences as she ran her fingers through her hair and then say them out loud to me. And I would write them; they were always pragmatic, discussing essential matters with my eldest brother or Uncle Madhavan, Achan's, my father's, younger brother.

Dear Govindankutty . . .
Dear Madhavan . . .

I used to write letters to Achan on her behalf as well. She did not address him in them. There was no need to read them back to her. Amma would dictate them with such precision. At the end, she would write her name, 'Ammalu' and sign, 'A'.

When I was in college, she did not feel the need to write to me. Every now and then I would send her a postcard, to which I did not expect a reply.

I have spoken about Amma in some of my stories, those which are set in the period after our family began to encounter difficulties.

My elder brother had described to me a time when Amma had enjoyed great prestige in the village. She used to undergo courses of Ayurvedic treatment such as *navara kizhi*, *dhara* and oil massage whenever she stayed in Achan's ancestral house in Punnayoorkkulam. Achan had a good position in Ceylon. He was the eldest son. The sojourn of the eldest son's wife in her husband's house, concern for her health and well-being: these were matters Achan's family considered important.

Amma's health was not very good at the time she conceived me. The village *vaidyan* decided that she must have an abortion and she was given medicines to abort the foetus. But they did not have the desired effect. I arrived, probably because it was in my destiny to be born. I was not a healthy child. And Amma's health remained in grave danger. Which was why she was prescribed a complicated regime of treatment.

The flat wooden bathtub used for oil massage and the vessels meant for preparing medicinal brews had been lying idle for a long time till then in the attic in Achan's house. Every year, courses of treatment were conducted for Amma. Achan was not living in his village at this time, but the instructions he sent were never disregarded.

When coming back home after Amma's treatment, we would take a boat from the Uppungal ferry and go by the Cannolly canal to the Beeyam bund. Arrangements were made for Amma to lie down comfortably in the boat. We would get off at Beeyam and proceed to Kudallur in a cart drawn by two bullocks.

I do not remember those boat rides. I only know of them through my elder brothers' descriptions.

During the Second World War, Achan did not come home for five years. I wrote a story, 'In Your Memory', about how he came home after that period accompanied by a little girl.

I am not certain that she was his daughter. There was talk of her being the daughter of a woman in Ceylon by her first husband. Going through some old letters, my brothers discovered later that Achan had a son while he was in Ceylon and that his name was Prabhakaran. Balettan, my elder brother, confirmed this when he went to Ceylon without Achan's permission to look for a job there after he finished his college studies and stayed above Achan's place of business.

The little girl, whose name was Leela, stayed in Achan's house in Punnayoorkkulam for about two months. She used to wander around the place with my cousin Karthiyayani oppu. The writer Kamala Das, whom we called Aami, met her there and once told me she remembered her.

Amma, however, distanced herself from Achan after this incident. The latter would visit us in Kudallur every time he came home, that was all. He always stayed longer in his own house in Punnayoorkkulam. Amma would not go there. The letters she wrote to Achan were very formal and mostly about expenses. There will be an additional expense next month; this time, we will need to buy rice. Things like that.

Amma had studied under the local village teacher, the *ezhuthacchan*. I heard her mention it on occasions when she squabbled with her younger sister: 'I had an adequate education. I've even studied the *Amarakosham*.' When Amma was a child, there were sixty-four people in her *tharavad*, the house where the joint family lived, including children and grown-ups. An ezhuthacchan was accommodated in a room downstairs in the pathayappura to teach the children. They were taught texts up to the level of the *Amarakosham,* the Sanskrit thesaurus.

Uncle Achu, the senior-most male member of the joint family, had the reputation of being a fierce man. Whatever knowledge I have of the time when this man ruled the house is gleaned from the bits and pieces my mother told me. When we were children, it was Amma herself who reigned over our branch of the family, both my uncles being younger than her.

Amma told me stories about my ancestors: about Uncle Porayan, who died in our *padippura*, gatehouse, after eating poisoned chicken and Uncle Thassan who hoarded the money he made from selling areca nuts, converted it to gold coins, buried the coins and then lost his mind and spent his time digging for them since he could no longer recall where they were buried. My grandmother had seen all these ancestors of mine.

Gradually, the household began to encounter more and more hardships. We were distanced from Achan. Amma started to wear a serious look all the time. Achan's younger brother quarrelled with his nieces and nephews and came away from his own house, bringing nothing with him; his wife looked continually distressed and, to make things worse, had fits every now and then. Amma and she often squabbled about trivial things, but they loved each other deeply. This aunt died when she was over ninety. Whenever she spoke of her elder sister, her eyes always filled with tears.

There was nothing Amma enjoyed more than cooking and serving large groups of people. She always had someone to help her with the housework, young girls or women who had broken away from their families after the partition of the property. The family who lived on the northern side of our house were the children of a distant uncle. One of them often came over in the daytime to help Amma. There was hardly enough food in our kitchen to offer helpers like these a hearty meal. None of them expected any compensation. Rather, they vied with one another to come over and assist Amma because they knew of her generosity.

I never saw Amma or her younger sister going to temples to pray, as people in the village usually do. Nor did they have a bath early morning and make marks on their foreheads with sandal paste. Indeed, they preferred to bathe in the evening.

In the years when the harvest was fairly good, there would be just enough paddy to last us through the year. If the rains failed, Mithunam and Karkitakam would be months of severe scarcity and we would have to borrow paddy. Despite this, Amma always loved having people over. A relative called Kuttettan used to often spend the night in our house. He would tell the children stories from the epics. Achuthan Nair, who had quarrelled with his wife, his sister and all his relatives and now lived alone at Kaithamparabath, would visit us every now and then too. He and Kuttettan made it a habit to sleep on the front veranda. Once they finished work, Amma's assistants would crowd behind the door of the *thekkini*, the southern room, while Amma herself would sit on the front veranda, leaning against the wall. She did not speak much. Kuttettan and Achuthan Nair would have gathered all kinds of news from the village, and Amma enjoyed persuading them to relate everything they knew to us.

Amma spun out her own account of her journey to Ceylon over several days. Bits and pieces of the voyage she made from Dhanushkodi to Talaimannar still linger in my mind.

As soon as Kuttettan stubbed out his palm-leaf torch on the ground to extinguish it and then came and sat down on the veranda, Amma would say to him: 'Have a little something to eat, Kutta . . .'

'I had dinner before I came, Malu.'

'We managed to get four paral fish. There's some gravy left. Lay a leaf, girl.'

Kuttettan never refused a meal if he knew there was fish curry. And there were always guests at home irrespective of whether the stock of paddy was diminishing, or whether the money from Ceylon was late. Amma would never let on even if times were difficult. It was only during Onam that she would deign to borrow some money, and the hardest hearts in the village would loan her cash if she asked.

Sometimes, I would be told to go and bring her the cash. Amma never went anywhere herself, not even if Kunjathol of Mankoth illam invited her to her house. Once she had the money she needed, she would entrust it to Uncle Kuttan, her brother. She would already have decided how to spend it, what to buy, for whom to buy clothes and all that.

I would often receive a warm welcome from Chozhiyath Achuthan Nair, infamously called the 'Cobra' in our village, when I went to borrow money from him. It was indicative of how much he respected Amma—the way he asked after my family and offered me buttermilk every time I was there. When I was enrolled in the First Form in Kumaranallur High School, Amma decided it was not right to make me walk such a distance every day. So, she rented a small house closer to the school. 'The children can avoid walking to school at least until the rains abate,' she said. There was me and my elder brother, Kochunni ettan. Our relative, Gopi ettan, was sent from the village to help us. He cooked for us, but we never thought of him as a servant. Chathu Nair succeeded him. Amma came over occasionally and stayed for three or four days. She soon made the acquaintance of a young girl who lived next door, Parukutty. The girl began to come home to help Amma. She would comb Amma's hair and rub medicinal powder into her scalp. Amma did not like Chathu Nair's cooking, so Parukutty started to cook for us under Amma's supervision. Chathu Nair left, saying he would come back after a week. 'I have work to do in my garden.'

'He has absolutely no work in the garden,' said Amma. 'He's upset that Parukutty is doing the cooking. He won't eat what she cooks!' Parukutty was from one of the so-called inferior castes. Amma would say: 'My mother didn't care as long as we were neat and clean.'

She did not believe in the rules of caste.

'It's his cooking that disgusts me! He has betel leaves in his mouth all the time. And why can't he wash that soot-covered dhoti? He never does, the wretch!'

The year there was a cyclone, Abubakker and his family came to our courtyard and called out for help, but my brothers were reluctant to open the front door. In our household, no one ever entered through the front door if a woman in the house was having her period because Bhagavathi, the Mother Goddess, resided in our *machu*, the attic. However, Amma said there was no need to observe such rules in times of calamity and opened the front door.

Amma was taken for treatment to Madras in January 1953. It was cancer. She was not aware of the seriousness of the disease. My eldest brother, whom I called Valiettan, went with her. From my college in Palakkad, I went to the Olavakkode station to see her. They had spread a sheet for her to lie on in the sleeper compartment of the train. Amma was seated with her legs stretched out, leaning against a pillow. Valiettan tried hard to conceal his distress. Just before the train moved out, she took something out from the corner of her dhoti and handed it to me. It was a rupee note. That was all the money Amma had. Many years later, I wrote about this incident in a story called 'Seeds'.

Amma was brought back home after a month. I was then preparing for my exams. I went on a morning train to see her and returned by evening. I couldn't bear to see her lying in bed, her fair skin turned sallow and dark, and her stout figure reduced to skin and bones. She could not speak. She looked at me for a while and then closed her eyes.

It was amid my exams that the letter from Valiettan arrived.

The letter, written in English, began: 'Dear boy, be prepared to hear the worst.'

Amma had died the night before.

I was told that I did not have to go home at once. It was enough if I participated in the funeral rituals on the fourteenth day. 'Write your papers with care,' the letter said.

The outlines of the portrait of Amma that have taken shape through a few stories of mine are actually very incomplete.

At the time when our tharavad property was divided, there was no one to argue on behalf of the section of the joint family to which Amma and her children belonged. Her younger brothers were not old enough to speak for her. Amma and her three small children were given a piece of land that could be cultivated. One of my older aunts had married early; her husband was a man of means and they moved to the house he had built. My grandmother and the family moved to a small hut in my aunt's compound. After that, all of us moved to a little house on the hillside. It was called 'Chettippura' because a Chetty family that made *pappadam*s used to live there. From there, we moved to the pathayappura in the tharavad.

Eventually, Amma bought this pathayappura with the money she had accumulated from the sums Achan sent her and later, the *nalukettu* as well.

I have been told that I was born in the hut in my aunt's garden in Kothalangode.

I remember very little of my childhood in Chettippura, but I remember the time we spent in the pathayappura of the tharavad more clearly. When the property was finally divided among Amma and my uncles, there were no arguments. None of the uncles wanted the family residence; they only wanted the land. If Amma wished to buy some land at the current rate in the village, they told her she could do so. No one was leaving the house for good. Amma said it would be best if proper documents were drafted.

There was only one point that she insisted on. There had to be five shares in Amma's portion, not four. 'The house and compound are not meant only for my children,' she said. 'They are boys, after all. My younger sister, Kunjukutty, has a daughter. She is entitled to one of the five shares, exactly like my children.'

The tradition in our village was to expand property inch by inch, gently dislodging the earth at the boundary lines with a spade. People would argue fiercely over whether a mango tree had fallen on this side of the boundary or that; it would end in their stabbing each other! Later, the people in the village praised Amma's decision. To give away a one-fifth share was no small gesture.

I began to write a bit after I finished high school. Some of my elder brother's work had been published by then. I worked hard on my writing during the vacation. Amma had no idea what we did upstairs in the pathayappura. And although some of what I wrote came out in print, no one told Amma about it. Valiettan's wife, whom I called Edathi Amma, was the only person who read what I wrote. Anyway, Amma would not have been interested even if she knew. She never asked us about the marks we scored in our exams. Burdened as she was with domestic problems, she did not pay attention to trivial things. She was sure her children would study well and pass their exams and didn't need to know beyond that.

Once during my college vacation, Amma saw me searching in her wooden box.

'What do you want?' she asked.

'An *anna*. Or even three-quarters. To send a letter.' I needed a three-quarter anna coin to send a literary creation by book post.

'There's nothing there. There's some change in the betel box downstairs, take what you want from that.'

As children, we had no bad habits. You would laugh if you knew: drinking tea outside of our homes was considered a bad habit in those days!

My uncles Kuttan and Achu were afraid of Amma. Uncle Achu would never climb into the veranda without stubbing his bidi on the ground to put it out.

Uncle Achu and Ayyappan, our Harijan worker, once had an argument in the fields. They carried it into the toddy shop. The news that Uncle had beaten up Ayyappan reached our house. Amma was aware that Uncle Achu sometimes went to a toddy shop. But he never came home intoxicated or reeking of alcohol, so she did not bother about his drinking. Amma was fond of Achu's wife and children. She would scold Uncle if she felt he was not paying enough attention to the family matters that concerned them.

However, the day she heard about Uncle Achu's quarrel with Ayyappan, Amma's reaction was quite different.

Before Uncle could start to explain, she said, 'Go and apologize to him. Don't enter the house again until you do so.'

Uncle Achu hesitated.

Amma continued, 'Do you ever go to the fields? Has Kuttan ever gone by them since he became the manager at the *Illam*? It's thanks to Ayyappan that three or four sheaves of paddy arrive here to be threshed every time the months of Kanni and Makaram come around.'

Her brother realized it was futile to argue with her.

Uncle Kumaran, who belonged to another branch of our family, was well known for his expertise in drafting land deeds. Ever since Uncle Achu started to work as his assistant, he received small sums of money as remuneration.

'Do you have any money?' asked Amma.

Uncle Achu was hurt. 'Do you think that I slapped Ayyappan that hard? When he resisted, it was my hand that was injured. People had to drag him away quickly.'

'All you need to do now is listen to what I say.'

Uncle walked to the hilltop in the darkness.

Ayyappan had a sturdy frame. He could shoulder a load normally carried by three people. When there was work to be done in the fields, he would labour until dusk and the other workers would curse him. When we moved to a house in Kumaranallur, it was he who hoisted all our packets and bundles on his head and accompanied us.

Amma would scold Ayyappan often, on days when his wife, Neeli, came and whispered in her ear in secret.

'If I hear that you came home drunk and beat her up, you will not be allowed to cross the gate and come and work for us.'

For several days after that, Ayyappan would be on his best behaviour.

If Amma came to know that any of our neighbours were out of rice, she would send them small quantities of the rice she had pounded from borrowed paddy. Her younger sister would mutter angrily that Amma was needlessly generous.

'Do you want to give away everything we have? Even the children are having only rice gruel for lunch these days.'

When my aunt heard about an ungrateful person Amma had helped, she told everyone about it. Amma listened quietly and then said, 'Kunjukutty, you won't remember an incident about when we all went to Rayaranelloor. You were a baby at the time. When we arrived there, we saw a child sitting all by himself on a hilltop, crying. My aunt said piteously, "Oh, look at that poor thing, sitting all by himself," and the child looked directly at her and retorted, "Poor indeed! It's your old man that's poor."' Amma smiled as she said this story. 'That is how some react, but it does not mean that all will react in the same way.'

Amma left us too quickly. Her younger sister, who lived till ninety, is gone too. Two of my brothers have gone. Uncle Kuttan and Uncle Achu passed, one after the other.

The celebrated mother who addressed me as her 'dear son', who wrote me a letter scolding and blessing me in the same breath, is gone as well. I have the photograph that Vaishakh brought before me. As I gaze at it, I hear Amma ask, 'Why do you speak of these old wives' tales now, child?'

Why? Because I had to, Amma.

A group of people here, my good friends, have discovered that I have turned seventy. They want to clothe me in the blankets and sweaters of old age. But I suddenly wish I could go back to the time when I was a little child sitting at your feet, Amma. That is why I had to say all these things about you to my friends.

I have still not said everything I wanted to. There is so much more that remains to be said. I shall put all of it away carefully.

I know you will forgive me, Amma.

3

A Story Is Born

My friends, I find it difficult to answer your question: how does a story take shape?

A very famous American literary figure was asked by his admirers: 'How is it that you have been able to write so many novels?' The writer, whose works had an excellent market and who earned more than a dollar for every word he wrote, replied, 'I go and sit before my typewriter and curse myself soundly.'

I have heard of people who carry out the creation of a literary work as if it is an office job, working for a specific number of hours every day. I am envious of them.

For the moment, let us ignore the statement, 'more than a dollar for every word'. We need to do this to maintain the mental well-being of our writers. Still, if we are to be honest, there is on the one hand a greed for money and on the other, the pressure exerted by newspaper persons—it starts with their appeals and ends with threats. Every day, I go home promising myself firmly that I will not rest until I write a story. Unclear and sometimes very clear themes could be drifting through my mind at this time. I sit down, a sheet of beautiful white paper in front of me and the Parker pen that was once a character in a story of mine, in my hand. I look as if I am just about to write a story. I curse myself not once but a hundred times. I write 'A Short Story' on one corner of the sheet, scrawl my name below three or four times both in English and Malayalam, think some more, curse myself again. All the pressures, all the greed, become futile—nothing comes to mind. Not that there is no story within me. Sometimes, I write reams. But as I spin out sentences, the thought strikes me that I am deceiving myself. In the end, filled with a resentment directed at no one in particular, I get up and creep under the mosquito net, where sleep enters without being cursed.

And so ends my endeavour to write. At other times, I have rejoiced in writing effortlessly, and without having begun with an aim to do so.

When is one really able to write a story? And how does one manage to write it? It is impossible to explain.

Sometimes, it is when you curl up in your chair, letting idleness take over your senses, that the idea for a story darts unexpectedly into your mind. You may lie in bed, thinking about all kinds of things and remember innumerable incidents you have seen or heard. Moments when you wept soundlessly or smiled painfully rise in your heart and glide towards you. Sometimes, the people around you are transformed, and characters you created have taken their place. And your mind moves into a state of turbulence. Once this happens, a story that had never occurred to you before takes shape in your mind. I think most of my stories came about in this way. Their characters, utterances, their surroundings, movements, the expressions—all take shape before you gradually. At this point in time, you begin to think about form, about concentration. By the time you have built up your ideas, bound them together, unbound them, made comparisons and taken decisions, the story will be clear, its form complete—the beginning, the end, even the title. Once you reach this point, you can assure yourself that a story has been born. And you can then transfer it to paper whenever you please.

There is the possibility that you may depict absolutely unplanned events in a story you had already written out fully in your mind. And you will be convinced later that the deviations that suddenly appeared in it are appropriate. I think that in a story in which almost every detail has been carefully thought out before, sections that find their way into it, thanks to these sudden impulses, have a particular charm of their own.

The germ of a story, an idea that occurs to you quite by chance like a vague gleam of light: the intellectual and imaginative activities that nurture its growth do not obey the rules of convenience or necessity.

There are no general rules to follow when writing a story. Perhaps a general law can be formulated: that it is essential you enter the womb of a story. While I am busy with other things, I take comfort in telling myself that I will write a great deal when the vacation starts. But what inevitably happens is that I painfully watch the vacation I had intended to spend in splendid literary activity pass by in futile daydreaming. In short, none of my best-laid plans for writing were ever executed.

Over a certain period, I read the Bible over and over again, night after night, with no specific aim. Its words and sentences and the events it described stayed in my mind.

One day, when I woke up feeling resentful towards the whole world, I saw the Bible that I had been reading the day before in front of me. I turned its pages and wandered a long time with the Son of man. I thought about Jesus and Judas and the world in general. Probably because a deception of which I had recently been a victim had embittered me, the thought of the thirty pieces of silver haunted me. What if Jesus had met Judas again? I imagined Jesus resurrected, walking with Judas over the deserts and cities of Central East Asia. The surroundings were full of smoke, of the echoes of bullets. I picked up a piece of paper and began to write and finished a story in three hours: 'When Flowers Bloom in Akeldama'.

On many occasions like this I was able to write, thanks to sudden impulses. I have never felt the need to go in search of the encouragement to write without experiencing the labour pains that writers speak of as an adornment to the art of writing. Often, the word 'encouragement' as I hear it used today seems a fake coin to me.

One day, as I thought about my village, I remembered a woman named Meenakshi, who belonged to a branch of our extended family, the members of which had moved away after our property was partitioned. She eventually died by suicide. My thoughts drifted around her for a while and a story emerged effortlessly from them, without any great mental exertion: 'Kuttiedathi'.

Oftentimes, stories written with great intent can fail unutterably, while those written spontaneously, can be great successes. Like I said, it's impossible to lay down any kind of general rule.

Let me share a moment of truth with you at this point: when I started to write this book, my aim was to say something about story writing in general and then describe, step by step, how a particular story took shape. I had decided to use 'Iruttinte Atmavu' (The Soul of Darkness), a story I like, for this purpose and had analysed the mental activity that had gone into writing it. I can never forget its protagonist, the madman Velayudhan. The wooden pillar in the house north of mine to which he used to be tied has now been completely devoured by termites. But the image of Velayudhan—I should call him Velayudhettan since he was older than I—dragging himself around the pillar with broken chains on his feet is still clear in my memory.

But I suddenly feel compelled now to write about another story: 'In Your Memory'. I think I must have written about a hundred stories in all, good and bad. But the only time I wept after I finished writing a story was when I wrote 'In Your Memory'. I cannot define the precise stages in which it took shape. However, I can clearly recall the anguish I experienced while writing it. I do not have any sisters, and this was a sorrow to me when I was a child. I used to long for a sister.

When I was ten, Achan came home from Ceylon after an absence of four years. Everyone at home had been eagerly awaiting his arrival, especially my elder brothers, Amma and I. When he arrived, there was a little girl with him, a fair-skinned girl who spoke only Sinhalese. We all froze when she entered the house through the front veranda with Achan. The air around us filled with all kinds of suspicions. Some whispered that she was Achan's daughter; others said a friend of his had been killed when a bomb exploded in Ceylon and that Achan had brought back this friend's orphaned child. What was the truth?

Even today, I do not know for sure. But I felt she was Achan's daughter. She had to be because she would then become my sister.

I was the only person who was happy about the situation. The ambience in the household changed. People were quick to pick quarrels, there was constant muttering and murmuring, occasional sobs, some gentle words of comfort. After a few days, the little girl went back with Achan. Memories of that child lay in my heart for a long time, then gradually faded. As I grew up, I ceased to think about her. Achan came home many times after that. The scars of old quarrels healed.

In June 1954, someone said to me in a lowered voice, as if it was a secret: 'I heard that the girl who came here with your father got married long ago.' I did not ask him how he came to learn of this. We were in the street when he spoke to me, I was on my way to attend a wedding. As I walked on that crowded road, heavy with the odour of tobacco, noisy with voices that spoke a Malayalam tinged with a Tamil accent, a picture took shape dimly behind a curtain of memory. Of a little girl seated on a steel trunk, twirling a key on a chain.

Meanwhile, we arrived at the house where my friend's sister's wedding was taking place. I sat by myself in the crowded hall, watching the ceremony. My friend was running around, fulfilling his various responsibilities, exchanging small talk with people, giving orders. My thoughts slipped back to the old picture in my mind. My friend's sister's wedding was happening here. And there, in that place far away, my sister—I had never abandoned that childhood concept—had celebrated a wedding ceremony like the one I was watching now.

As I left the wedding house filled with troubled thoughts, I made a decision. I would write a story about the girl's groom. Events from the past kept surfacing in my mind. I could visualize the people who had taken part in them. If I was going to write a story, my mother would be a character in it. I thought of Amma, who had died a year ago. I walked back to the college hostel. The students were reading, and I was supposed to supervise them. Instead, I walked to my room, closed the door and sat down at my table. I had to write that story at once.

I went back to that night when a conflict had torn the family. All I had to do was search for the images that lay buried deep in my memory and organize them. A noisy crowd of visitors that had gathered on the front veranda, a gramophone playing on one side (the object called a gramophone had arrived in our house for the first time). Upstairs, however, in the room above the veranda, Amma and Achan faced each other angrily. Words exploded, shattering the air. Downstairs, in one corner of the thekkini, a little girl sat on a tin trunk, newly arrived in a world that, to her, was filled with wonders, looking stunned, unable to understand what was happening around her.

A climax could be worked out from that scene. It would start with Achan's arrival and end with his departure from the house. Achan, Amma and the little Sinhalese girl: these were my characters.

When I sat down to write, I suddenly realized that the members of my family had deliberately chosen to forget the events I was going to describe. None of them would wish to speak about them. And when Achan read this story, my courage drained. What would the others say? There was already an accusation against me, that I constantly wrote stories about people in my family.

My next attempt was to try and write the story from some other standpoint. If I did not feature in it, then it could pass off as a story that had happened to some other family. A husband, a wife and a child he had allegedly fathered with another woman. I tried to create new surroundings for them. There were so many stories about a suspicious wife. But I gave up, tore up whatever I had written and went to bed.

I forgot about writing the story, but the sister I had met as a child came to mind again. I remember that night still, the night when I wove images from memory and from my imagination together, the picture I had of the girl leaving the house with Achan. Troubled, I got up, then sat down to write again.

I would tell the whole story, hiding nothing. Let whoever wanted recognize the incident.

I thought about the three characters again. From whose viewpoint would I write?

A writer can narrate events exactly as they happened, situating himself in the world in which they took place. This is the simplest technique in story writing. Using a third-person narration is convenient to explain things when needed or to lower or heighten the speed of events. But this technique would not suit my story. What was important was not the events themselves but the mental conflicts of the people who were involved in them. Therefore, the story had to be told from the point of view of one of the characters and I had to choose the viewpoint of the most important character.

Whom would I choose?

The Sinhalese girl was the pivot of the story. But it would be difficult to enter her thoughts and her emotions. She was not a character I could control; I knew nothing of the landscape of her life, of how her emotions had evolved.

Amma would make a great protagonist. A woman desperate for a daughter, offering prayers in temples for one, now faced with a little girl who steps into her evenly paced household, upsetting its balance and rhythm. Achan would also be an excellent character, a man torn and agonized by contradictory loves in his life.

What if 'I' became the chief character? The character 'I' was a ten-year-old boy; I saw him very clearly before me. A boy in red shorts, standing bewildered against the murky background of a deeply disturbed family. One moment, he was happy because the sister he had always longed for had come to his house. But the next moment, he was saddened to see the members of his family quarrelling with one another because of her. All he could do was look at his sister from a distance. He was afraid to go up to her and anyway, she would not understand what he said. She wears a beautiful dress and smells fragrant, while he is clad in shabby shorts.

. . . *I could hear his heart beating rapidly.*

Yes, I would narrate the story through my eyes. The shoot of tenderness that had sprouted in my heart as a response to those events . . . I would use a simple, lucid style, suited to the nature of a child. If I wrote it as a reminiscence, then I would be able to use the language of deeply felt emotions, its explosions, its violent storms, its volcano-like eruptions of fury. However, that was a style I detested. And since I would be describing what a ten-year-old boy had seen and heard, such a style would not be suitable either.

I wrote the date on top. At that moment, I peered back into the past and wrote the first sentence: 'After many, many years, I suddenly thought of Leela today. Tomorrow is her wedding day.' I am not sure these were the exact words, but that is more or less how I started.

Readers would assume that it was another of those mournful stories written by a man disappointed in love, on the day before the girl he loved got married. It was usual for stories about unrequited love to begin that way. I thought readers should not have occasion to misunderstand Leela at the very beginning. No one likes my heroines now. Readers complain that all of them have heavy hips and full breasts. I did not score out what I had written, however. So that the meaning would not be ambiguous, I continued: 'Let me tell you in advance, lest you misunderstand, she is my sister.'

I then plunged ten years backwards into the past.

When I wrote at the end: 'My beloved sister, from miles away, I send you my blessings,' my eyes were full of tears. I wrote the title, 'A Page from Life'. Later, when the story was published in a book, I changed the title to 'In Your Memory'.

When I lay down to sleep that night, a sense of fulfilment flooded my heart, for I had finished writing a story that had caused me deeper pain as it took shape, than any others I had written.

4

The Festival Season

When I was a child, the temple festivals in our area were very grand. There was the *thalapoli* festival in Chamminikkavu, featuring a long procession of young girls carrying platters of small oil lamps that have been lighted and auspicious objects, and the Chirankara and Kalladathoor *vela* festivals in honour of Bhagavathi, the Mother Goddess, with splendidly caparisoned elephants and percussion. The festival that took place nearest to us was the Malamakkavu thalapoli. Our village temple, which had nearly crumbled, was renovated recently and a festival is conducted there every year. Good fortune has come once again to our Vazhavil Bhagavathi.

The Ariyambadath Temple, however, remains the same. I always found the *koothumadam,* where *koothu* performances were held, very attractive. We used to walk through the temple compound to board the bus to Aloor.

In those days, the Ariyambadath festival did not compete with the festivals in the neighbouring temples. Its special feature was that it conducted koothu performances

over ten continuous days, using leather puppets. Uncle
Kuttan had a passion for this art form. He would come
home at dusk and announce, 'Let's go for koothu. If any of
the children want to come, they can.'

None of the adults were interested, and I was the
only one among the children who wanted to go. There
were two girls from the house next door, however, who
would arrive by way of the garden to accompany us,
waving palm-leaf torches. We would set out after dinner.
By the time we crossed the fields and reached the road,
a half-dozen men and women would be waiting. Uncle
must have let them know earlier that we were going. The
women would have screwpine-leaf mats tucked under
their arms.

Ariyambadam was quite nearby—a mile and a half
away according to the way distance was calculated at
that time.

We would find twenty-odd people already seated
on mats in front of the performers. There was never the
ambience of a grand festival—just a small boy selling
peanuts by the yellow glow of a chimney lamp and a tea
shop with a temporary palm-leaf screen. Neither of them
expected much business. Since not many children came, no
sweets or sherbets were sold.

The story was that of the Ramayana. It was later that
I discovered the verses they recited were from Kambar's
Ramayana. I listened attentively to the songs of the koothu
poets and watched the movements of the puppets. Hovering
drowsily on the edge of sleep, I would suddenly be wide
awake with a start when they came to the battle scenes.

From time to time, the koothu poets would stop
narrating the story of the Ramayana and speak about

the feast they had had that day, the hospitality they had enjoyed. Uncle Kuttan told us that they sometimes used a tone of mockery.

Uncle knew the performers well. Every day, a small audience would gather eagerly in front of the koothumadam. It was cold in the month of Makaram, and yet, they would sit there until well past midnight.

I enjoyed the return journey even more than the performance. There would be a tinge of cold in the air and innumerable stars that looked like a thousand tiny lighted firecrackers clinging to the clear sky.

All temple festivals have developed into great events now. With numerous elephants, fireworks that cost huge amounts of money and countless participants in the percussion. People want to make sure well ahead of the dates when each professional troupe will perform a play. Meanwhile, old cultural shows are languishing. Since there are few people left who can make bull-images with lifelike heads and straw-filled bodies, there are not many bull festivals. The *thira* and *poothan,* heralds of the temple festivals whose roles were done by men of the washerman caste, make only a nominal appearance now. The thira wore a heavy wooden, elaborately carved headdress and the poothan a mask, and once they finished their dance, a man carrying a sack—who accompanied them—would collect the paddy we had kept aside for them on a winnowing tray. The area where the thalapoli procession of the Malamakkavu temple used to be held is now divided into small plots, with dwellings in each of them. The festival itself is now celebrated in the Ayyappan temple below.

The arrival of the Mookan Chathan marks the start of the festival. 'Ah, the Malamakkavu festival is about to begin!' The *poothan*s arrive next. Nowadays, one can still find poothans and thiras but the *pana-poothan*, the *chavattila-poothan* and the *para-poothan* have all but disappeared. Among the para-poothans, I have seen the *karimkali* dancer mostly in the Vanneri area. He first bites into the neck of a live rooster, and then performs with a blood-stained mouth. The days go by swiftly until the day of the thalapoli: the beauty parade of the time. It was a rule that the young girls from all the houses in that area should carry platters in the procession. As they saw the faces of the young girls in the radiance of the wicks glowing brightly on each platter, discreet enquiries would be made: 'Who is the girl in the red blouse? The one who is third in the line?' It was not uncommon for someone to visit that girl's house a few days later bearing a marriage proposal.

All communities used to take part in these festivals. Young Muslim boys worked enthusiastically at spots where fireworks were being organized or water distributed.

Festivals have now turned into competitions—between temples and between committees. Between communities, because the festival in the mosque has to be celebrated on a grander scale than the one in the temple. Festivals in which all the communities in the village took part have disappeared.

Since the dilapidated Vazhavil temple in my village has now been repaired, a festival is held there every year. But only hints of old customs and rituals remain: two or three bulls, two or three poothans and thiras. The thalapoli used to be conducted exclusively by the higher castes and one of the happy changes that have come about is that all castes now participate in it. My Malu oppu (Valiamma's daughter), who is over eighty now, used to carry a platter in the thalapoli procession until very recently to maintain an old tradition. She is sad that her health no longer permits her to do so.

The character of festivals has also changed. And much has been lost with change. Many old rituals are no longer performed and cultural features peculiar to each village have disappeared, just like the way the Ariyambadath koothumadam has crumbled away and become part of the fields that surround it.

5

Those Who Told Me Stories

I believe there is an old Hasidic saying, that God created human beings because he liked to listen to stories.

Is there anyone in Kerala today who recalls a writer named Variath Kuttirama Menon? Quite by chance, I met his daughter and her husband in Goa a few years ago. They were astonished when I told them that I had not only heard of Kuttirama Menon but had read his stories with great enthusiasm.

Some of his stories had appeared in the *Mathrubhumi* weekly magazine. The characters that featured in them were rats, cats and owls. There were many illustrations. My favourite story was 'Darikan's Journey around the World'. I think it was published in four or five parts. The grown-ups read all the stories and poems first, and I had to wait for the weekly until they had finished with it. The story goes something like this: A baby rat named Darikan comes out of its hole at night and wanders around the yard and the compound of the house. While doing so, it encounters many dangers and escapes death by a hair's breadth from all of them. One of the chapters ends with a frightful enemy getting ready for action. I was afraid for Darikan, very anxious and sad, but I nursed a hope deep within me that the following week he would escape. I waited impatiently for the next issue.

When I was a little older, one of my teachers at Kumaranalloor High School, Vasunni Nambiar, guided me into the wonderful world of stories. He was from the neighbouring village, Malamakkavu. He did not actually teach our class. The teacher who had been appointed to do so had not started to work at the school, and Nambiar, who came instead, decided not to begin a lesson for us since the teacher appointed to our class would eventually arrive. With the preface, 'I'll tell you a story,' he began to narrate *The Count of Monte Cristo*. Names such as Edmond Dantès struck me as odd, but a few minutes after he started to narrate the story, all of us were captivated by Dantès. The period came to an end just as he was being arrested and taken away when he was about to get married. We sat stunned.

What would happen to him?

We wished then that the teacher who had been appointed to take our class would not make an appearance too soon. The story continued to unfold and went on until Dantès escaped from the isolated prison on the island. At that point, the new teacher arrived.

We wanted to hear the rest of the story. Nambiar always started for school late every morning and walked very fast to get there in time. But when returning home in the evening, he would take his time. We would crowd around him, anxious to hear the rest of the story. Our master would walk through the jamun forests and over the Parakkulam hill, then through several lanes, narrating the story.

After he finished *Monte Cristo,* he began *The Three Musketeers:* Athos, Porthos and Aramis, so different from one another in nature, and Count d'Artagnan, who came from the village to join the king's bodyguard, the real hero. They saved the king and queen from the wily conspiracies of Cardinal Richelieu. Ah! their journey to recover the necklace that the queen had presented to her old lover, the King of England. The method the cardinal had devised to disgrace the queen was to reveal her secret. The king commands her to appear in court wearing the celebrated jewel. The cardinal makes plans to secretly imprison each of the travellers on their journey.

Their intrepid journey, their escapes—we prayed for those courageous warriors. We battled side by side with them, transforming into minor warriors in Dumas's reckless world. The story was never finished.

One of my distant uncles, Koorthavalappil Kuttan, was an expert on the epics. He had separated from his wife and children much earlier and lived with his sister and her children. He used to come and sleep in our house at night. Although there was not much water in the river in summer, there was always plenty under the Karunoor bridge, at the spot where the Kunti River joined the Bharathappuzha. Uncle Kuttan would tell us stories as we walked to the river to bathe. He knew of every scandal, every slanderous episode in the village, but they were for the family audience. For us children, there were stories from the epics.

I remember how in my ignorance, I once hurt Uncle while he was telling us the legend associated with the installation of a temple that had fallen into ruins.

'As they cut through the forest of thickets and reached the southern tip, just imagine, they found a Shivalingam there!'

'A Shivalingam—that means . . .'

'A Shivalingam, that's it. A Shivalingam.'

It was not clear to me. Was it a statue or an idol? But Uncle Kuttan hurried ahead with the story, unwilling to be trapped.

None of those stories from the epics have stayed in my memory. But a story that Uncle Kuttan narrated to us in great detail found its way into my heart: the story of Palat Raman. Uncle described the scene in which Unniyamma's brothers, hearing that Unniyamma was with Raman in the bathing pond, surrounded the pond, their swords unsheathed. But all they could see was Unniyamma standing by herself in the pond in water that was waist deep. Raman was hidden under her long hair!

I thought of the young girls who bathed in the illam pond, their thick, heavy hair undone. A girl had to have very thick hair for a grown man to be able to hide inside it. I discovered the secret truth—that a child like me could easily hide inside Bhargavi's or Janaky's hair.

The days when I had been so worried about Athos and his gang, whom our teacher had told us about, had come to an end. When I started to read on my own, I sat awake all night reading *The Count of Monte Cristo,* a book that was seven hundred pages long. I read *The Three Musketeers, Twenty Years After* and *The Man in the Iron Mask.*

R. Krishnan, a doctor and the son of my friend, was an admirer of *The Three Musketeers.* Four or five years ago, I went to Krishnan's house for the usual medical check-up before going on a trip abroad. I discovered then that there were admirers of Dumas in the new generation as well. What was more, a boy gave me the name of a book I had not come across. I wrote it down and searched for it but did not find it.

While sorting out my books, I came upon an old and unabridged edition of *The Three Musketeers* and thought it worth a re-read. I was surprised to find that the old excitement had dimmed, and I could no longer participate with the same childlike passion in their defeats and victories.

What had happened?

As time went by, rough rock-surfaces must have taken shape in my mind over its old innocence. The cruel conspiracies devised by the old cardinal no longer upset me. My heart no longer kept company with the brave warriors. I no longer adored the queen.

Recently, I read the English translation of the Syrian writer Ulfat Idilbi's Arabic novel, *Grandfather's Tale,* which she wrote at the age of seventy-nine. The novel is about a mother telling her children a story that her grandfather once narrated to her. She uses her grandfather's words. It did not surprise me that a writer who had done research on *The Thousand and One Nights* should have adopted this narrative style.

Somewhere, people must still be telling stories. And there must be listeners. I read in a travelogue that old people in the tribal settlements in the deserts of Jordan often used to narrate stories at night. It is common in these regions to demand grain, silks and camels as bride price when negotiating a marriage. It is said that over the last few years, a television set is included in this list of demands. Maybe in time there will no longer be anyone to listen to the stories that grandfathers and grandmothers tell.

There are no storytellers like Uncle Kuttan in the village now. Nor are there likely to be teachers who narrate stories to their students.

It is thanks to people such as Variath Kuttirama Menon, Vasunni Nambiar Master and Uncle Kuttan that I began to scribble stories in the pages of a notebook by the light of a lamp lighted at dusk, with a silent prayer that someone somewhere would read them. My salutations to them!

6

A Place for Books to Live In

Then, as now, Thrissur has always been a town famed for its jewellery. The establishments of old advertise their wares. There is a sentence at the bottom of each advertisement: write for a free catalogue.

At home, it was my task to go to the post office every evening. I would feel sorry for myself because nothing addressed to me ever arrived. And then I saw this sentence. I sent a card to the advertiser. Would they dispatch a catalogue if they realized the request for it was in a child's handwriting?

A thick catalogue addressed to me arrived in a few days from Unniyattil Kuttan Menon Company. A catalogue with pictures of gold ornaments. The women passed it from hand to hand. It found its place in someone's trunk as a document that might prove useful on some future date.

Palakkad and Kozhikode were towns that had a close relationship with our village. For the people of Punnayoorkkulam, where Achan's ancestral house was, Thrissur was a city of wonders. I too longed to see

Thrissur, for some children who had visited the zoo and museum there had described their marvels to me. It was the only place where one could see the rare snake called a *rajavembala*, the king cobra.

Valiettan, my eldest brother, became a teacher at Valappad High School. When he moved there, the family sent word that they would visit him one Saturday and Sunday. All three of us, his younger brothers, went to Valappad. On our way, we stopped at Thrissur and visited the museum before we boarded the bus to Valappad.

As I grew older, Thrissur attracted me increasingly because many famous writers lived there, in the shade of Mangalodayam Press. The poet Changampuzha Krishna Pillai was among them and those were the days when the lines from his poem *Ramanan* echoed through our villages. Basheer lived in Thrissur, Thakazhi and Keshava Dev often visited the place. The town was the literary critic Joseph Mundasserry's headquarters. I had a vague notion about the halo that encircled Appan Thamburan. Mangalodayam Press published works of all the well-known Malayalam writers of that time. Later, Basheer and many others would write that A.K.T.K.M. Vasudevan Namboodiripad was not merely a publisher, he was also a guardian to all writers. Several writers came to reside in Thrissur because of the close relationship they had with him.

I never tired of going through Mangalodayam's catalogue of books for hours on end. It listed the works of every writer I admired. But how would I ever find a way to buy those books? And then, while I was in the tenth class, I was awarded a scholarship. I was given seventy-two rupees towards the scholarship for the previous year as well. M.T. Narayanan (M.T.N.) Nair (Kochunni ettan), the brother who was immediately older than me, and I spent days making a list of the books we could buy with this money. We wanted at least a few books by every well-known writer. Most of Changampuzha's books cost only eight annas each. G. Sankara Kurup's play *Iruttinu Munbe* (Before the Darkness) cost eight annas. A rupee for Basheer's *Invaluable Moment*. A rupee and a half for Thakazhi's *Friends*. We compiled a long list, leaving out all books that cost two rupees or more. Kochunni ettan undertook the responsibility of buying the books, which remained part of our family library for a very long time.

I wanted to join Kerala Varma College after completing my Secondary School Leaving Certificate exams. Anyone who dreamt of being a writer had to find their way to Thrissur, and in particular to Shree Kerala Varma College, which boasted teachers such as N.V. Krishna Varier and E.K. Narayanan Potti, the author of *Sahithya Darsanam*. The renowned professor, poet, critic and scholar Sankaran Nambiar was the principal of the college.

Meanwhile, the members of my household were discussing the question of whether they could send me to college at all. No one came up with anything definite. The problem was, of course, insufficient finances. In the end, I went on my own to Thrissur and found out where Kerala Varma College was. I asked for N.V. Krishna Varier, the reputed poet, scholar and editor, but he was not there that day. I then made some enquiries and discovered that admissions had been closed. On my way back home, I went to Mangalodayam Press and spent a long time looking at all the books there. I left without buying anything since all I had was the bus fare to get home.

Vadakke Koottala Narayanankutty Nair, commonly known in Kerala as V.K.N, has written innumerable amusing stories about the merchants in the Thrissur market. The Thrissur dialect became a part of the comic element in cinema. I read Sara Joseph's novel *Aalahayude Penmakkal* (Daughters of Alaha), recently and really enjoyed the roughness, the beauty and the comic quality of that dialect.

The old Mangalodayam Press gradually fell into decay and when Thomas, Mundasserry's son, started Current Books on a small scale, he came to me saying he wanted to publish a collection of my short stories—the fourth one, 'In Your Memory', with Devan's cover illustration. Later, Thomas's Current Books published several books of mine. Thanks to Current Thomas, my relationship with the town of Thrissur grew steadily stronger. Thomas upheld the old tradition of the publisher as the writer's guardian. On the occasions when he visited me in Kozhikode, he often tried to persuade me to buy ten cents of land in Thrissur and build a house there.

A friend from Thrissur said to me: 'I have fifty cents of land, find me a buyer and I'll give you the ten cents you want at cost price. I don't want a profit.' This person was Popular Chakunni, whom I first met as a friend of P. Bhaskaran and who died a premature death.

Thomas approved of this idea. Claiming to be an expert in building houses, he agreed to the plan. He calculated my royalties and decided to build the house in two stages within two years. But he gradually moved from publishing to other areas of business, and I was upset. One day, when I received a cheque for a small sum from Thomas's office together with a note informing me that my royalty account had been closed, I was devastated. I made some enquiries and was told that Thomas was travelling through Andhra on business. I was suddenly in a situation where I had to search for a new dwelling for my books and dispatch those children of mine to places I did not like.

Around that time, Thomas's son, Peppin, began to publish again and after a few years, Thomas's wife, Saramma, asked if I could do something to help them. 'Let me think about it,' I said hesitantly, haunted by the memory of how my books had been orphaned. Young Peppin insisted that he seriously intended to run the publishing firm well and I finally gave in. The volumes that had been in the old Current Books returned to Thrissur one by one, like tame pigeons that had come back home after taking flight.

My good friend, the writer Sethu, wrote from Mangalore when he heard that I was going to take on the responsibility of the Sahitya Akademi: 'I was in the Akademi for three years. I felt at that time that everyone who walked through the marketplace in Thrissur believed their day was not complete unless they had thrown a stone at the Akademi. Therefore, beware!'

However, it is not for its Akademis or its Pooram-festival spectacles that I love this town. The first time a beautifully printed book I had authored looked out of its glass case and smiled at the world was from a small bookstall in it.

Do not Thakazhi, Changampuzha, Basheer, Mundasserry and all their companions gather to sit and talk in the shade of Thekkinkad Maidan during the hours when it lies deserted? In the glow of the lamp posts of a distant past, I still glimpse the long shadows of all those who once walked there, searching for one right word to follow another.

7

The Nila River I Remember

In 1954, Edasserry Govindan Nair, who illumined the paths of Malayalam literature with his great poetic prowess, was stunned when he came to know that the bridge across the Bharathapuzha had been completed. He then wrote 'Kuttippuram Palam' (The Kuttippuram Bridge), a celebrated work that has been quoted time again in discussions that relate to the environment in Malayalam poetry and aesthetics. The poet praised the sculptural grandeur of the bridge. Twenty-three lakh rupees had been spent on it, a sum that was by no means despicable at that time. The poet visualized the thousands of vehicles flying over the new pathway with his inner eye. But he did not conceal a sharp fear that the purity of the villages on the banks of the river would disappear in the near future. The poem ends on a note of doubt:

Mother, great river, will you turn
Into a filthy gutter?

The Bharathapuzha, known also by its pet names, Peraaru and Nila, has not only turned into a gutter, but in fact, faced a far worse fate. The poet did not foresee the dangers of the massive thefts of sand from the riverbank, nor the state it has fallen into now, the desert wasteland that it has become. In several spots, huge thickets have grown over little mounds of river sand. You can even see casuarina trees growing in the middle of the river in the area between Kuttippuram and Thirunavaya. Only for a few days during the rainy season are these trees submerged at least partially.

The Nila was an inspiration to many of our great poets, including Vallathol, P. Kunhiraman Nair and Edasserry. For the common people, this river will always remain the pure Dakshina Ganga (The Ganga of the South). Vallathol established his renowned institution, the Kerala Kalamandalam, in the village of Cheruthuruthy on the banks of this river. Innumerable artistes—writers, musicians and Kathakali dancers—come from the countless villages situated on its banks, from Kalpathi to Ponnani. Because of this, it has been continuously described as the great source of the cultural flow in Malabar.

I saw the Peraaru in one of its most fearful forms during the floods of 1942 and 1944. We were secure in our tharavad since it had been built in a compound that was at a much higher level than the paddy fields. I have heard the elders say that the floods of 1924 were even more frightening, that the water came up to the foothills that time.

I clearly remember the floods of 1944. I was dispatched in the afternoon to buy something from the provision store. Instead of coming back home by the short route through the fields, I chose to return by the path that ran

along the bank of the river. The river was full to the point
of overflowing and looked fearful. Some older people,
stationed at various spots on that route, waiting for me to
reach home, kept crying out, 'Run, Vasu, run, the water is
rising very fast . . .' By the time I ran with all the speed I
could muster and reached the gate of the house, the water
had risen above the level of the road and was surging into
the fields. It kept rushing in like this for four whole days.
Many of our relatives, close and distant, vacated their
houses on the riverbank and took shelter in ours.

We used to have our baths standing on the steps below
our padippura. On days when it rained very heavily, the
river would hiss threateningly all day that it would overflow
its banks any second and spread all around us; all night,
it would scream the same threat. But we were never afraid
of the river. The dark hill ranges in the distance and the
rain clouds that rolled up towards the sky gave us all the
warning we needed.

Life in the low-lying areas was completely devastated
by floods. The rising waters ruined the banana trees and
vegetable patches that farmers surreptitiously cultivated
on the banks of the river. Ordinarily, the villagers used to
leave the two sides of the river untouched since they were
susceptible to flooding. This helped lessen the force of the
flood and gave the earth and slush that was rich in manure
a chance to settle.

At one period, the Bharathappuzha was useful for
transport plying between Palakkad and Ponnani. Double
boats would speed towards the Ponnani harbour, carrying
agricultural products. They would often spend the nights
on our riverbank. The boatmen would light fires on the
bank and cook food. Standing in our yard, we could hear

their friendly squabbles until late into the night. Once in a while a Mapilla song would waft into the peaceful ambience of the night.

In the summer, everyone, except the very old, bathed in the river. Although the water in the bathing ponds was shallow, it did not feel as pleasant as the fast-flowing, crystal-clear water in the river. Families who did not have wells used to dig pits on the riverbank so that they could have pure water in their houses.

During summer, guests and relatives came in hordes from distant villages and from towns such as Kozhikode and Thrissur to the wealthy houses in our village. It was an occasion for our young men to steal furtive glances at the fashionable women who went down at dusk to the river with the elders in their families to have a bath.

Cattle bathed in the river as well. They had special bathing ghats to walk into after gruelling work on red-hot summer days. Children were considered sufficiently mature by the elders if they could lead cattle down to the water without allowing them a chance to nibble at the shoots growing in the paddy fields on either side of the path. (Just as they were considered to have completed their studies in Malayalam once they could read Thunchath Ezhuthacchan's *Ramayanam* without fumbling over a single word!)

In summer, the river lying bathed in moonlight was like a radiantly glowing dream to me, though it has become a very distant memory now. None of us were allowed to go near it since it was considered the favourite playground of ghosts and devils and of demigods such as *yaksha*s, *kinnara*s and *gandharva*s. Villagers who alighted at the train station late at night crossed the river with the utmost caution. All those who inhabited the earth and the sky believed that if you did not give these ghosts and demigods any trouble, they would not bother you either.

You had to cross the river and walk six kilometres to get to our family deity, who resided in the Kodikunnath Kavu temple. All of us believed implicitly in the legend associated with her.

Long, long ago, our family consisted of a very poor widow and her three children. The old woman reared cows. Every morning, she would cross the river and deliver milk to the temple. In return, she was given enough rice for the day. Once, during the monsoon, the river flooded, and the boatman did not have the courage to ply his boat. Unable to cross the river, the widow returned home and told her children that they would get no rice until the water receded. She warmed some milk, gave it to them and put them to sleep. At midnight, she heard a knock on the door. When she opened it, the widow saw an old woman, completely shrouded in dripping wet clothes, standing there. This guest who had appeared at such an untimely hour placed a bell-metal vessel filled with rice in front of the widow and commanded her: 'Wake up the children and feed them!' She disappeared immediately.

On the fourth day, when the water receded, the widow went to the temple as usual with milk. She took the bell-metal vessel with her, intending to tell the priest what had happened. The priest was taken aback. A bell-metal vessel which was always kept inside the sanctum sanctorum had been missing for the last three days!

We grew up loving and worshipping the Devi (Mother) who had brought our hungry grandmother and her starving children food at midnight, in the pouring rain. We have another grandmother as well, the mother of our Kodikunnath Kavilamma. She is the deity of the Muthassiyar Kavu temple, near Pattambi.

According to legend, the grandmother and her three beautiful daughters (one of whom was Kodikunnath Kavilamma) wandered along the banks of the Nila one summer night. They stopped to watch a Harijan festival and enjoy its profusion of songs and dances. The youngest daughter was so captivated by the whole spectacle that she refused to go back with the others. The mother then asked her to stay with the Harijan folk and be their guardian.

This is the origin of the Kanakkar Kavu temple.

On another occasion, the other two daughters began to quarrel while watching an animal sacrifice. The younger one was fascinated by the bloodshed. The older one abandoned her and settled down at Kodikunnath, while the younger one went away to Kodungalloor. We all know that blood sacrifices performed in Kodungalloor was banned several years ago.

Today, hundreds of trucks are parked at every spot, in every panchayat and on every path on the banks of this river. Paths have been dug right down to the middle of the river bed by people who want to take piles of sand out. The thickets that began to sprout at several spots have grown into little forests. Because of these forests, cardplayers who while away hours in the daytime on the banks of the river as well as distillers who brew illicit liquor at night are no longer easily visible to the world outside.

If you pass through the villages on the banks of the river in the months of Medam, you will see women lined up, waiting patiently with plastic pots of many colours for trucks carrying drinking water to arrive. The level of the groundwater in the region has descended so low that the wells in the vicinity of the river have dried up completely.

The Bharathappuzha set the stage for many battles and historical events such as the Mamangam in olden times. Violent fights still break out on its banks, incited by controversies regarding the limits to which sand can be mined, or the weight of the loads that each truck can carry, or the various possibilities that each licence issued may offer and so on. Interminably long rows of huge trucks are packed tightly into every available path to the river and its wide expanse will never be visible again. All one can see is the pathetic sight of pits dug everywhere to scoop out the sand.

The Nila River was for us a most gracious and merciful mother. It was she who guarded and caressed our secret dreams. Now, it pulls into its depths the despair and shame of our children whom evil destiny has led astray. Loved ones who died used to accept the funeral rites we performed for them with this mother of ours as witness. And that is how they went peacefully to the other world.

The Nila River which inspired me so deeply, which forgave the conflicts within me with such grace, which bore witness to my passage to adulthood, now draws her dying breath . . .

I feel as if someone is slicing into the veins of a profound maternal love. A colourful past, a perfection tinged with nostalgia, all its cultural traditions are slipping away from our village. Yes, we are gradually losing all of it, almost all.

8

The Second Footfall

I could not fight the nausea and threw up even before I
got to the potted plants. It was not bile. When I saw that
it was blood from my insides, I was shocked. Fear swept
over me.

I walked forward slowly, hiding my anxiety. I reached
the portico, where my friends were gathered. I found it
difficult to talk. When I got up a second time, feeling
uneasy, I could not make it to more than four feet ahead
of me. The dark, almost blackish stream that spurted
out from me, tearing out the roots from somewhere deep
inside, bathed the plants in red. The odour of blood spread
rapidly around us.

Someone within me made swift calculations and
whispered: 'You fool, it's time!'

Two cars speed to the hospital over a road on which the
street lights have just begun to glow. Potfuls of my blood

fall and break repeatedly on a road that keeps alternately running ahead of me, then fading . . .

This was surely the end. Perhaps everything would be over suddenly. I felt no fear, no grief. A profound sense of peace, devoid of emotion, filled my heart.

The car went right up to the hospital veranda and stopped. My friends supported me as I tried to get out.

Don't become so helpless, don't, commanded my mind.

'Please, I'll walk . . .'

What a relief! I could talk.

They must have telephoned earlier. Nurses in nuns' robes were waiting for us. However, when I put my foot forward and tried to walk, I realized my legs were lifeless. My friends caught me as I collapsed.

'A wheelchair, a wheelchair!' someone called out.

The wheelchair slid into the depths of darkness. My eyes made an effort to capture the light from the lamps on the veranda but failed. By the time I sank down on the bed in the hospital room, demons of darkness had rushed out from a tunnel and encircled me.

When I came to myself, there was a doctor I knew well with me and nurses. And my good friends from the city as well. What day was it? The day I was brought in or the day after that?

'I had heard that the mind grows empty in extra-sensory meditation. I was certainly in a state of emptiness. Never before or never after did I experience this condition when my mind, completely unburdened, raced haphazardly.

The doctor spoke words of comfort, but I caught only a few bits and pieces—words such as 'disease' and 'death' that first came close to me, then slipped away into the distance.

'Let him sleep. Let him sleep longer,' the doctor advised.

My friends followed him to an outer room.

It was then that I saw him. Obviously a villager, he stood in a corner of the room, a bag hanging from his hand. Since everyone had left the room, he approached me slowly.

Who was he?

I attempted a smile.

'I . . . I am Balakrishnan.'

A few uncertain moments passed and then I remembered Balakrishnan Ezhuthacchan from Vadakkanchery.

'I read the news in the papers and started out at once.'

I had never forgotten the occasion when Balakrishnan first came to see me. He had marched into my house one afternoon, looking every inch a villager, humble and respectful, with nothing that was artificial about him. And yet, I was suspicious: had he come with some sob story, to ask me for money? Or was he from my village or its vicinity, some man with a medical problem?

'I just wanted to meet you. I am Balakrishnan.'

He was a farmer. He had a wife and two young daughters.

'I've been wanting to come and see you for a long time. But I'm a farmer and there's always some work or other that I must attend to every day. I could not get away until now.'

He wanted nothing from me. Nor had he any advice to give. He had none of the characteristics that those who described themselves as appreciative readers or admirers usually possessed.

In fact, Balakrishnan had nothing much to say. He was a small-time farmer but made enough to live on. He had no interest in any of the pastimes common to villages in the interior, such as getting together in a group or scandal-mongering. What he really liked was to read. He bought books.

This was the sum of the bits and pieces he told me.

After a while, Balakrishnan made ready to go. I asked myself, *Should I not give this pure-hearted reader something towards his fare?* I pondered over this. Then I saw him take out some worn and shabby notes from his pocket and crumple them up in his hand. I was stunned when he held them out in both hands towards me.

'What is this?' I asked.

'You must take it, please don't say you won't.'

I felt weak. 'Look, Balakrishnan, I'm not hard up. I have a job. I have no financial problems at all.'

'I know all that. But when we go to a temple, do we not give money as *dakshina* to the priest or as a gift to the temple? Think of this as that kind of a gesture.'

I felt helpless. Balakrishnan insisted I accept the money. As he was about to leave, I signalled to him, 'Wait. Let me see if any of my books are here. Please wait.'

'I have all of them, there's not one I haven't bought.' He gave me a gentle smile and left.

It was the same Balakrishnan Ezhuthacchan who stood before me now.

'When I read in *Thrissur Express* . . .'

I attempted a smile again.

'Are you feeling better?'

Every now and then, one of my companions came in and told me that I must try and sleep. The day ended between sleep and wakefulness.

When I opened my eyes once and realized where I was, I noticed that Balakrishnan was still there, by my bed.

'You haven't left?'

'I came prepared to stay. I've arranged for someone to take care of the work on the farm.'

'Look, I'm feeling better. You go along, Balakrishnan.' Balakrishnan stood there with his head bent. 'There are lots of people here, this is a good nursing home.'

'I know. Still, if you need to go to the toilet or the latrine, isn't it awkward since all the nurses are women? I'll stay. It's no trouble at all. That's why I came.'

The bag in his hand had clothes and other necessities.

I was firm with him. I would tell someone to write to him if I needed him. Weren't his wife and children on their own on the farm? I told him sternly that he had to get home before dark.

Balakrishnan left reluctantly.

Someone asked me who the visitor was.

'A person from my village,' was all I said.

Death was still lurking in the corridor outside. Balakrishnan's footfalls grew fainter and fainter. I wept that day for the first time since I fell ill, carefully, so that no one saw me.

Balakrishnan had gone away, leaving by my bedside, like invisible talismans, the invaluable seconds of a segment of time during which I had learned the truth of expressions I had used very casually when I was young, expressions like 'the sorrow of love'.

Here was a man who had loved me only for the words I had written. Once I had begun to earn a livelihood with the words I wrote, people had doled out felicitations, rebukes and curses to me in varying measures. But this kind of love, this emotion was something I had never experienced. It astonished me.

I closed my eyes, contented with the peace and comfort of the knowledge that words were not completely useless.

9

The Man Who Helps People Die

Disease, death, an accident: whatever the event, the first person the Kudallur folk went in search of was our relative Padmanabhettan. Though perpetually drunk and intoxicated, he would at once take on all responsibility for whatever had to be done. He would go down to the river, have a bath, drape the dhoti that he had tucked into the rafters of one of the huts on the riverside around his waist, smear *vibhuti* on his forehead, arrive at the appointed place and take charge of everything. If it was a house waiting for a death to happen, he would spend days there. The people of the house would have to persuade him to eat. Once the impending event or the cremation was over, he would leave. He accepted money only if he was very close to the people in the house and would go directly to the toddy shop with it. Surprisingly, Padmanabhettan could get arrack on credit even if he had no money.

Padmanabhettan was the son of one of my distant uncles. He had never married. When his family property was divided years earlier, he had got a small coconut grove as his share. He sold it and entrusted the money to someone. He used to take out small sums from this amount on credit. He was not at all upset when, at some point, he found out that the money had given out.

For quite some time, he used to sleep in the house of one of my older aunts. She never showed him the least discourtesy. However, he eventually moved to the veranda of a shop because he wanted to be independent. Then, when a bus shelter was built in the village, he moved into it. When people turned up to wait for the morning bus, he would still be asleep.

Up until his last days, Padmanabhettan's attitude remained exactly the same as it had been when I was a child. Sometimes, he visited the houses of two or three persons he was very close to, to borrow money and one of these was my tharavad house. He feared and respected my eldest brother, Valiettan, who often scolded him. But severe as he was, Valiettan would often give him some money even though he knew that Padmanabhettan would go straight to the arrack shop with it.

The fact was that no one could dislike Padmanabhettan.

A boy in our family who had been ill for a long time finally died. At night. It was raining heavily. My brothers told me that Padmanabhettan was the only person who turned up at once to help.

Padmanabhettan always came to see me as soon as he knew that I had come home. He never ate in our house, even when we tried hard to persuade him to. All he wanted was some money, but he would never ask for it. He would just hang around and it was impossible not to give him some. If I was staying for quite some time, he would reappear after a couple of days.

Valiettan usually sent Padmanabhettan to the Kodikunnath temple once a month to make offerings on our behalf. Ettan would send for him a day ahead and he would come early next morning after a bath, his forehead smeared with vibhuti. He would cross the river, walk the six or seven kilometres to the temple, make arrangements for the offerings and be back by nine in the morning. He would hand over the receipts for the offerings, the *prasadam* and the exact amount of cash that remained.

Six years ago, I arrived in the village one night. The next morning, Padmanabhettan arrived even before I got up, freshly bathed, ready to take Valiettan's offerings to the temple. I too gave him some money for offerings on my behalf.

When he came back, he said to me as he gave me the prasadam from the temple, 'Vasu, I think the old woman is displeased.'

I did not understand.

'The coconut we offered did not break into two clean halves. You had better go there yourself.'

The 'old woman' he meant was the Kodikunnath Bhagavathi, the deity of the temple. He was an ardent devotee of hers. The villagers used to say that, in the days when he had been a *pagida* player, when he threw the dice down at a decisive moment, the numbers on them would add up to the precise figure he needed. Everyone believed that it was the Kodikunnath Bhagavathi who helped him on such occasions.

When I came to the village one summer, I decided to walk to Kodikunnath in the evening. It was a roundabout route by car, about twenty kilometres. As we set out in a small group, someone cried out, 'How awful! Look, who's that lying there?'

It was Padmanabhettan, lying by the roadside.

When we got back at dusk, Uncle Raghavan told us that Padmanabhettan was dead. Someone had gone up to where he was lying, to tell him to get up and move to the shade, only to discover that he was dead. No one knew exactly when he had died. Had he been dead when we had left? None of us had gone up to him, since seeing him lying asleep had been such a common sight in our village.

That night, Raghavan and some others cremated him by the river.

Padmanabhettan knew all the rites and rituals connected with death. When the moment of death was imminent, he would advise the relatives about the last life-breaths, the *oordhvan* and the *chinnan*. He would calculate the time of death well ahead according to the stars and the segments of the lunar months and tell the relatives discreetly when they could expect the event to happen. It was said that on most occasions, Padmanabhettan's calculations proved correct.

When I wrote the story 'Swargam Thurakunna Samayam' (When the Doors of Heaven Open), I had in mind Padmanabhettan, who conducted the ritual of helping people die so beautifully. Fearing that someone would tell him this, I called the character in the story Kuttinarayanan. In the story, Kuttinarayanan's calculations fail in Master's case. This story was the starting point of the screenplay I wrote for the film *Aalkkoottathil Thaniye* (Alone in the Crowd). Master and his children became the chief characters in the film, but Kuttinarayanan has an important role in it as well.

Someone asks Kuttinarayanan as he bathes and gets ready for the funeral rites of a person who has just died, 'Who will do all this for you, Kuttinarayanan, when you are about to die?'

'I . . . when I die . . .' Never having thought about such a situation, Kuttinarayanan feels helpless and very upset. The actor Kuthiravattam Pappu played this role extremely well.

There are still so many stories to tell about the village and Padmanabhettan may well feature in some of them. For there is only a part of Padmanabhettan in Kuttinarayanan. A small part of a big character.

SECTION II
STORIES

10

Seeds

'. . . And some fell among thorns and the thorns sprang up and choked them.'

Amma's brother, who had taken his share of the property and gone away, came to the house one evening and scolded Amma loudly. When her son Unni sprang up, his blood boiling, to answer back, Amma said to him, 'He's talking nonsense, Unni, why take him seriously?'

Amma was seated on the veranda when she said this, running her fingers through the pepper-and-salt strands of her hair, circular gold earrings hanging from her elongated earlobes.

The veranda was plunged in darkness.

Huddled on the steps of the pathayappura, Unni thought, Amma, I've come back again.

The hurricane lamp hanging on the hook in front of the house swayed gently in the breeze. The shadow of the bell-shaped *kathirkkola* that hung from the middle of the roof of the veranda moved up and down the wall opposite. It must have been hung in the month of Chingam the year before.

All the paddy grains had slipped out, but it continued to hang there as an ornament. No, Unni corrected himself— not as an ornament but rather in the nature of a custom.

The house and its neighbourhood usually lay asleep at this hour. But today there was a clamour as lamps and people scurried to and fro. There were commands, the clatter of vessels and the sounds of people calling out to one another. A ritual repeated every year.

Achan was seated on his chair in the circle of shadow beneath the lamp, smoking a cheroot. His face lay in darkness and shadows. In the glow of the cheroot, only the glint of his spectacles could be seen.

Moonlight gleamed over the courtyard smeared with cow dung.

Achan cleared his throat. 'Hasn't Ayyappan come?'

'No.'

'The train left long ago.'

Unni made an indistinct sound.

Clattering noisily over the bridge, the train that was known as 'the eight-thirty' had passed that way earlier and Raghavan was supposed to have arrived on it.

'Did Raghavan write to you?' asked Achan.

'Yes, a few days ago.'

A lie. There had been no letter from his brother Raghavettan. A New Year card arrived regularly once a year, with Raghavettan's signature in an elegant hand below the lifeless printed letters that unstintingly wished him health and prosperity.

Raghavettan used to write to him regularly when he was in college. The letters would be full of advice. 'You must get a First Class. And then write the Indian Administrative

Service examination. You can do it if you try hard. Your past achievements prove you can do it.'

He thought of the anniversary functions held in the schoolyard and of the crowds of people who gathered for them. He remembered the silk curtain with a picture of Goddess Saraswathi playing the veena on it, the coloured streamers rustling above his head, his teacher calling out his name.

Termites must have destroyed all the books he had received as prizes. They were lying now in the lidless steel trunk in a corner of the southern room upstairs.

Your past achievements prove you can do it!

'Are there any children as bright as he is?'

He had waited silently, listening to the praises, his body covered in goosebumps.

Unni will become a great man. The stars have destined it for him.

Raghavettan had stopped his studies after he repeatedly failed his examinations. Chandrettan, his other brother, was satisfied when he passed the tenth. His sister Ammini was after all a girl, so there was no need for her to study. Unni would study. He would write the IAS examination. He would rise to a high position.

In the end, he had become . . .

* * *

Inside, they were busy taking down the *paathi*, the flat wooden receptacle which was usually hung on the wall near the inner courtyard. People carrying lamps scurried in and out between the western yard and the house. Two persons came out carrying the huge paathi, accompanied by a man with a petromax to light their way.

'Shall we take it to the western veranda?'

'No. To the pond. Wash it now, quickly. Hurry, Govinda.'

Unni continued to sit where he was, on the steps of the pathayappura. The butt of the cheroot that Achan had thrown away flickered briefly in the courtyard, then died out as if shutting its eye.

'Could it be another train that passed by earlier?' asked Achan.

'No, it was the eight-thirty.'

'Raghavan should have arrived by now. Otherwise, he would have written.'

'Um . . .'

'Doesn't Ammini write to you?'

Unni grunted again.

Another lie. Ammini would not come this time. He had hoped to meet her when he came home. He had not yet seen his new nephew. The four of them lived far apart, in different places, but on Amma's insistence, they would meet on Onam and Vishu as a family.

On Thiruvonam day, five triangular banana leaves used to be laid on the long front veranda, the *nadappura*. Achan and his three sons would sit down before them, and a brass oil lamp would be lighted in front of the smallest leaf. In the old days, it was Amma who would serve them. Once Ammini grew up, she took over and Amma would stand nearby, leaning against the frame of the kitchen door and looking on.

They also followed orders to write to her every week.

'I am well. I had letters from Raghavettan and Ammini edathi. It's some time since I heard from Chandrettan.'

If this was all he wrote, Chandrettan would receive a letter from Amma three days later. 'I see that you have not written to Unni. What will you lose by writing to give him your news? You're all grown-up now, there's no need for me to tell you this.'

He realized now that it *had* been necessary for her to tell them.

It was not surprising that Raghavettan had abandoned them. He lived his life amidst account books and numbers. When timber trucks left the Nilambur forests for Kallai, currency notes would fall on Raghavettan's table. He eventually cleared the mortgage on the house and Chandrettan renovated the pathayappura.

Unni thought of how much lower he had sunk than all of them.

He heard Raji, the daughter of Chandrettan and Sharadedathi, crying upstairs.

Achan asked, 'Who's that crying?'

'Raji.'

'Why is she crying?'

'She's just being peevish.'

'She hasn't gone to bed?'

He heard Sharadedathi's voice: 'She wants the gramophone to be played. Obstinate girl!'

Chandrettan muttered a general statement about the obstinacy of children. Sliding his feet into wooden clogs, Achan said, 'Don't make her cry at this time of the night. Play her a couple of records if she wants.'

Achan began to walk up and down the courtyard. Unni got up and went to the western yard. There were lights and a lot of noise outside the pathayappura. The glare from the petromax lamp spilled into the banana grove on the other

side. Metal vessels clanged against one another. Young
men seated on mats told each other jokes in low voices and
laughed loudly as they grated coconuts.

Preparations for the feast the following day were in full
swing. He had seen feasts being prepared in this courtyard
so many times. Fireplaces had been built at this same spot
before his sister Ammini edathi's wedding. The cooks
had worked very hard. The day before Achan's sixtieth
birthday—Unni recalled that night, filled with lights and
commotion. Only one person who had rushed around
the house on the night when the serpent *thullal*s had been
conducted, giving everyone instructions, was not here now:
the face framed by wind-blown strands of pepper-and-salt
hair was no longer to be seen.

Someone made fun of the man who was stirring the
contents of a copper pot, wielding a long ladle with a
wooden handle. A loud outburst of laughter exploded
from the young men who were grating coconuts.

Preparations for an annual ritual.

It was Amma's death anniversary the following day
and he felt angry, with no one in particular.

He had no faith in these rituals—you made balls with
cooked rice, placed them on a leaf and clapped your hands
and the crows flew down and pecked at them. Probably
everyone believed that if the crows ate the rice, the hunger
of the human souls in the netherworld would be satisfied.
Still, when February came around on the calendar, he
always remembered that Amma's death anniversary was
approaching.

A card would arrive from Achan: 'It's Amma's
anniversary on the . . . [th]. I wrote to everyone today. I plan
to get there the day before, to observe the fast.'

He heard the grating sound of the gramophone as it began to play upstairs. A song from a Hindi film, filled with human and animal noises, slowly came to life. Chandrettan always brought a gramophone and records whenever he came. It was said that he carried them around wherever he went. Chandrettan was fortunate to have Sharadedathi as his wife, for she too was interested in music. Unni had often heard her sing *kirtanam*s beautifully at dusk. It was said that she had been an excellent singer in her schooldays.

Chandrettan always took his annual fifteen-day vacation when he came home for this death anniversary. There would be a festive ambience in the new pathayappura until he went back. The gramophone had no rest, day or night. Little Raji listened to film songs and learned them.

Achan called out: 'Unni!'

Unni went to the front courtyard.

'I see a light at the gate. It must be Raghavan. Flash your light on the steps.'

Unni stood by the withered rose-patch and peered over the wall at the gate. Ayyappan entered, waving a hurricane lamp. There was no one behind him.

'You're alone, Ayyappan?'

'What?'

Unni did not repeat what he had said. Putting down the hurricane lamp in the yard, Ayyappan cleared his throat.

'Ayyappa!' cried Achan.

'The young master was not on the train.'

'Were you at the station when the train came in?'

'I was. I waited there a long time after the train left.'

Kuttan Nair, the *karyasthan*, came out, placed his hand on the rafter of the lower veranda and asked, 'Hasn't he come?'

Achan did not say anything, so Unni answered for him, 'No.'

'He must be busy, otherwise he'd never miss the anniversary.'

Achan grunted. 'Kuttan, it's forty-one years since his father died and thirteen since my mother left us. Wherever I've been, I've never missed their anniversaries so far.'

'That's true. And that's how it should be.' Kuttan Nair laughed. He had an artful laugh. From the time he had arrived here as Achan's manager several years earlier, Unni had realized how skilfully Kuttan Nair could exploit that laugh to please Achan. He was no longer the manager now. But he always came over when Achan visited. He was content to be Achan's karyasthan again for a couple of days. Which meant listening to whatever Achan said, grunting his assent and laughing when necessary.

'There's one thing though, Master. Do you want to hear?'

Kuttan Nair called Achan 'Master'. My father was a teacher in elementary school in our village when he was young. Later, he left this job and the village and did well for himself. Although he did not go back to teaching, the appellation 'Master' continued to cling to him.

Unni had worked as a teacher as well, after he finished his studies and grew fed up of looking for a job or reading endlessly. For four months. He was still a teacher to some people. Recently, a young ticket examiner in a railway station had smiled at him and asked, 'Where to, Master?'

'To Palakkad. I don't recognize you.'

'You taught me in the fifth class, in high school.'

He recalled a pair of eyes filled with admiration from the days when he had been a teacher.

Kuttan Nair was describing Raghavettan's crowded work schedule. He had visited Rahghavettan once.

'So many coolies at work there! And timber being loaded and unloaded. He spends all his time on the telephone.'

The bright glare of a petromax lamp flooded the western veranda. Behind it came Achutha Kurup, the cook.

'What were you saying, Kuttettan?'

'I was talking about Raghavettan.'

'He hasn't yet arrived?'

'No. Ayyappan is back from the station.'

'He must be very busy.'

'That's just what I said. You would understand only if you visited him there. He doesn't have a moment's rest. "Sit down, Kuttan Nair, I'll be with you in a second," he'd say and go in. He would not come out again until dusk that evening. And in that time, drivers, merchants, all kinds of important people . . .'

Achan was pacing up and down, puffing at his cheroot but listening to it all. He loved listening to his children being praised, no matter by whom. If someone said Raghavettan was in a very good position, it meant that his father, Kuttanaserry Shekaran Nair, was in an excellent position as well.

Unni hovered in the shadows, leaning against the wall of the pathayappura. The sound of the gramophone upstairs had died down. Raji must have fallen asleep. Light poured out of the windows though, so he guessed Chandrettan was still awake. He was probably reading a film magazine or a crime novel.

This anniversary was an annual event for the siblings to get together. But neither Ammini nor Raghavettan had come this year. Another year, maybe Chandrettan wouldn't arrive. And what about himself?

Achutha Kurup was seated on the edge of the veranda, chewing betel. Looking up at the pathayappura, he asked, 'Haven't they gone to sleep yet?'

Kuttan Nair said, 'Eating early and going to bed by dusk—that's our way, isn't it? They're from the town. What time is it, Unni?'

'Ten-thirty . . . it must be eleven.'

Unni had had a watch when he was studying. It had worked until the year before. When he was told there was no use repairing it again, he had abandoned it. It had fulfilled its duties.

'Does Chandran have long leave?'

'He has to go back on the eleventh.'

Kurup said, 'He had to fast today. He must be very hungry.'

Kuttan Nair said consolingly, 'It's only for one day in the year.'

'True, but it's difficult for those who are not used to it. He's the sort who drinks coffee or tea every few minutes.'

Just as well Kuttan Nair had never visited Chandrettan at work, Unni thought, or he would have to listen to a description of his work schedule as well.

'Why didn't the child come?' He meant Ammini.

Achan said, 'Her husband could not get leave. So how could she have come?'

Unni went and sat down on the veranda, away from the glare of the petromax lamp.

Everything would be over by eleven the following day. If he left by the twelve o'clock train, he would be at the press by evening. The last form had to be put on the treadle at night. It would spit out the three thousand copies they needed only if Natesan Pillai trod the machine all night long.

None of them had seen him at work, they had no idea how busy he was.

The sun would be hot by the time he left, but the sand would not have begun to heat up as much. It would be impossible to cross the river in the afternoon. It was always at the moment of departure that he would feel he should not have come. Kuttan Nair, Ayyappan, Thami, the man who drew water, Kali, who swept the yard—all of them would be hovering around. Raghavettan and Chandrettan had made it a custom to give even the small children in the neighbourhood some money as they were leaving. At least a dozen people always accompanied them until they reached the river.

All he could give was a goodbye smile. *I must hold my head high*, he told himself. But then, he worked in a mediocre newspaper office.

May they never find out how little I earn . . .

'Kurup, have you finished your work?' Achan asked.

'I've chopped all the vegetables. The kalan curry is done. The boys are still grating coconuts. We can do the rest in the morning.'

'Kuttan!'

'Yes!'

'You must take special care when serving the outsiders. See that everyone has enough. I want the satisfaction of knowing that all the money I am spending has been used well.'

'Yes, but there's a problem. However much we cook, there is never enough for the outsiders. We cooked forty *para*-measures of rice for Amminikutty's wedding but still did not have enough to serve at the final round, when all the uninvited guests flocked in.'

'To say nothing of the bad name we earned . . .'

Achan said, 'Yes, that's all we got, a bad name. From next year, I am not going to serve a feast. We'll serve everyone kanji.'

Kurup said, 'That's a good idea. That's exactly what you should do.'

'You must finish everything quickly tomorrow, Kurup. I have much work to do.'

'Are you leaving tomorrow?' Kurup asked.

'Of course. Nearly forty men are at work in the fields and the cartmen will come to buy paddy. I won't have a moment's rest.'

Achan got up. Kuttan Nair called out: 'Chummukutty!' and the young girl, Chummukutty, who worked in the house came to the door. 'He's going to bed. Bring a lamp and take him upstairs.'

As the girl turned back inside, Kuttan Nair called out again: 'I've lowered the wick of the lantern Ayyappan brought and left it on the veranda. You can take that.'

The girl extended the wick in the lantern and picked it up. Unni caught a glimpse of the girl's face as she went in; she looked so much like Dakshayani. Dakshayani, Chummukutty's elder sister, used to come and help Amma with the housework. Large-eyed, she used to be a chatterbox. She lived next door and often came to play with Unni. Snot oozed steadily from her nose in those days. The two of them would draw lines and triangles on the ground with twigs on a spot next to the wall of the pathayappura and play *mukkuthu*. She was three or four months older than Unni.

He had seen Dakshayani earlier in the day, chopping firewood near the fence. She was twenty-six now. How could her vivacity have dimmed so quickly?

Achan called out from inside: 'Where will you sleep, Unni?'

'I'll sleep somewhere.'

'Go to the southern room upstairs.'

'All right.'

Unni heard footsteps, the bathroom door being opened noisily, Achan walking around upstairs.

Amma used to sleep in the room directly over the front room downstairs. After she died, her room was kept locked. Every year when Achan came, he slept in the room next to hers.

Amma's room was used only when Raghavettan visited with his wife and children. The large bell-metal spittoon shaped like a karaveera flower still stood under Amma's cot. The letterbox with brass fittings and the metal box which held land deeds were on a stool nearby. Unni wondered whether the old hand-held fan from which the gilt had worn off, the one that used to be tucked into a ring suspended from the ceiling, was still there.

He had spent many days as a child in that room, particularly on days when he had no school. His childhood scrawls remained on its walls; they had not been whitewashed since . . . There were surely some lines of Changampuzha's poetry . . . He had walked five miles to procure a handwritten copy of the poet's work, *Ramanan,* during his schooldays. He still remembered copying it into a hardback notebook in two days' time. The addresses of the newspaper offices that he had scribbled on the wall had not been effaced either.

Newspapers, books, writers—they had been his world. He had imagined that his goal in life was to attain that world. Now, he felt a deep sadness.

My beloved friends, you have never seen the tears in my heart.

Every year, when he came home, he went up to that room. There were bits and pieces of his past everywhere—on the walls, on the wooden ledge-seat, on the windows. On the eastern side, above the window next to the cot, he had written: 'On 14-11-46 . . . I saw . . .'

That was the day he had seen a poet who was dead now. It had seemed such a great event. He had seen him from quite a distance, standing on the sand-covered pathway as he was walking home one evening from a relative's house with a friend.

'What are you doing, sitting here like this?' Kuttan Nair came up, stroking his stomach. 'Isn't it time to go to bed?'

'I'm about to go . . .'

'You have to get up early in the morning. It's quite late already. Why do you look so dull and gloomy?'

Kuttan Nair sat down by him. Unni moved closer to the pillar and murmured, 'It's nothing.'

'Are you content to go on like this?'

He knew he was not. There was no point running a newspaper or writing. He had to make money, which meant that he had to join the timber trade. When trucks loaded with timber left the Nilambur forest and reached Kallai, currency notes fell on Raghavettan's table.

'Now is the time for you to really do something. You don't have any responsibilities. You should contribute to the family now.'

'Um . . .'

'Achan was speaking about you last night, Unni. At dusk, after he had said his prayers.'

He did not need to ask what Achan had said. About a son who had proved a dead loss!

He recalled Achan saying once: 'If I'd bought a coconut grove with the money I spent on educating him, we could at least have enjoyed the returns from it.'

Kuttan Nair advised: 'It's for your good that I say this: you must try and climb up, reach somewhere. Look at Raghavettan and Chandrettan.'

Unni grunted in reply.

After a while, Kuttan Nair said, 'Go to bed now, it's really late.'

Unni got up. The oil lamp that had been lighted in the southern room at dusk was still glowing bright. He went up the stairs. It was dark there. In the moonlight that filtered through the window, he could make out the cot and mattress, covered with Ammini's old red sari.

The door of the room opposite was open. He could hear Achan's loud snores. The sharp odour of his cheroot lingered on in the faint breeze that blew from the east into that room.

He felt suffocated in the low-roofed room despite the breeze. He caught sight of the closed window on the western wall. The latches were very tight. When he opened it, a blast of cool air poured in. Outside, the courtyard gleamed in the moonlight. A fire still blazed in the hearth the cooks had built in front of the pathayappura. He heard voices, probably from the bathing pond.

The serpent shrine, overgrown with trees and creepers, was a refuge of darkness. A little above it was the cremation ground. All the past generations reposed there and an isolated konna tree grew at the spot. It would be covered with golden flowers by the month of Meenam. The flowers of the burning ground . . . that could be a title for a poem.

He had slept in this room last year as well. He had looked out at the serpent shrine like this and watched the moonlight kiss the crest of the konna tree.

Last year, the house had been full of people. Ammini, Chandrettan and Raghavettan had come with their families.

He thought of Amma. She had been cremated under the konna tree.

Whenever he came here, he always thought of Amma, of her sitting on the veranda at night with her legs stretched out, chewing betel leaves, running her fingers through the strands of hair that covered her elongated earlobes.

The memory that surfaced most clearly in his mind whenever he thought of her was the incident of the rupee. That had been the day he first realized the nature of a pain born of love, and wept.

He had received a telegram saying that Amma was being taken to Madras. Raghavettan had sent the telegram and had mentioned the time of the train.

Unni waited on the platform. Even though the sun was hot, a cool breeze blew from the mountain ranges.

It was on this platform that he had first seen Gloria. He had stood here to wave goodbye to her. He had heard of Darjeeling, its great natural beauty, its lovely flowers, its lakes filled with blue water, its snow-covered peaks. Probably there were flowers growing around the military officer's house. She would look down into the bluish lakes and talk of amusing things . . .

He must forget . . .

The train arrived. He saw Amma's face at the window of a second-class compartment. Raghavettan sat facing her. A red blanket was spread over her seat and Amma was leaning back. The weakness and pain caused by the disease was plainly visible on her face.

'Don't you have to go to the office today?'

'Yes.'

All Amma knew was that all of them—Raghavettan, Chandrettan and Unni—worked in 'offices'. Amma had never seen his room strung with cobwebs, white ants scurrying over the bundles of paper piled up on the floor.

He stood on the platform, clutching the iron window bars. Raghavettan talked about what they would do in Madras. He had written ahead to some people. There would be no problem. The disease usually responded well to radium treatment. The doctor was excellent.

Amma could not speak very much. The eyes in the tired face, shadowed with pain, caressed him.

Raghavettan got down and went to the bookstall where English books were displayed.

'Unni, if you have work to do, you can go.'

'No, I don't have any work.'

After a while, Unni asked, 'Amma, do you want some tea or coffee?'

'No, I don't want anything. Don't stand there in the sun. Come in and sit down until the train starts moving.'

'No, it's all right.'

'I don't know when I'll be back from Madras. God knows.'

He longed to say something to comfort her. *You'll feel better with the radium treatment. This disease is not all that dreadful.* But he did not say anything.

He saw her undo the knot at the end of her upper cloth. She held out her hand and he took what she gave him. A silver rupee coin.

'For what, Amme?'

'Keep it, Unni. You're sure to find some use for it.'

He felt the years slipping from him. He was a small boy once more, standing next to the wooden money box, cracking his knuckles. Wearing shorts with straps, his unruly hair falling over his forehead . . .

As the train moved forward, strands of pepper-and-salt hair fluttered around her face.

* * *

Amma died.

Someone had knocked on Unni's door; it turned out be Kuttan Nair. With a letter from Chandrettan in his hand. He read the first sentence: 'Be prepared to hear the worst . . .'

He had arrived in the evening on the third day of the period of mourning. Achan was pacing in the yard. Both his brothers were there.

He felt he was entering an unfamiliar place. The house and its surroundings had grown very distant.

After that, all of them used to meet once a year. Every time he climbed over the stile at the entrance, he would think: It's been so long since I came here.

He lay with his eyes closed.

'Get up. The Elayad is here.' It was the Elayad who would conduct the rituals.

It was already daybreak, although it seemed as if he had closed his eyes just a minute earlier. The room was still dark. He went down and found the Elayad seated on a grass mat in the front veranda, chewing betel.

'Have your bath. We'll finish as quickly as possible.'

Achan had dragged his chair from the front room to the veranda and was reclining in it.

The *inangan,* a distant relative who had come to officiate at the rites, walked up to him. 'Everything is ready,' he said.

'Have your bath then,' repeated the Elayad.

Achan asked, 'Do you have a towel?'

'I'll get one from upstairs.'

'Chandran!' Achan called out. Then he caught sight of Raji climbing the steps up to the pathayappura. 'Raji, call your father.'

Raji stood at the spot where she was and called out in a feeble voice, 'Achan, Grandfather's calling you.'

Chandrettan came down the stairs.

'The Elayad is here. Have a bath and finish the rituals quickly.'

'I'm not having a bath.'

'What?'

'I don't feel well. I had a bad cold at night.'

Achan pondered for a while. 'All right then, don't bathe. The water in the pond is really cold. Unni is going to have a bath anyway, so he can perform the rites. That's all we need. Isn't that so, Elayad?'

'Yes, yes, that's all we need.'

Someone brought Unni a towel. He took some *umikkari* powder to clean his teeth from the container that hung from the roof and set off.

Kuttan Nair asked him, 'Are you going to the pond or the river?'

'The pond.'

Last year, the three of them had gone down to the pond together. Whenever the three brothers went out together while visiting the village, people working in the fields would stare at them in wonder. They saw the brothers only once a year. All of them worked in faraway places. All of them were educated.

'That lady did not have the good fortune to see them together like this.'

Unni came back in wet clothes and Achan said, 'Don't touch anyone now.'

Unni did not believe that touch could pollute. Everyone was polluted. And there was purity in everyone. He stood to one side.

The rituals were conducted in the veranda. Unni was familiar with them, he had performed them for quite a few years now.

The Elayad said, 'Wash your hands and feet and drape your dhoti in the ritual manner.' Unni pulled up the ends of his dhoti between his knees and tucked them into his waist at the back.

The brass oil lamp burned bright. The bell-metal *kindi* with a spout was full of water. Sesame seeds, karuka grass, thulasi flowers and sandal paste were all laid out on banana leaves. And butter and oil in small bowls. The inangan moved the copper water-pot to the side.

The Elayad started to intone verses. Unni had to do everything. If all the brothers were present, it was usually the eldest who performed most of the rituals. Chandrettan would stand next to Raghavettan, their bodies touching and Unni would stand with his shoulder touching Chandrettan's.

Unni knelt before the oil lamp. People were gathered behind the door, watching. Raji looked on, enjoying the wonder of it all as she sucked a red sweet. Unni could hear Achan say something in the front veranda. He sprinkled water silently on the floor and smeared cow dung over it. He laid the palm leaves in place.

The Elayad gave Unni instructions in a sing-song voice, and he obeyed them.

He had no faith in all this.

'Join your palms and make an obeisance before the lamp.'

'Pick up the sesame seeds, flowers and sandal paste, join your palms and worship the spirit of the departed person.'

'Sprinkle water on the tips of the karuka grass.'

Unni performed all the actions mechanically.

'Divide the sesame seeds, flowers and sandal paste into two portions, hold a portion in each hand and make an obeisance with your ancestors in mind. Sprinkle water three times.'

The souls of the dead would never come back into the karuka grass. He was sure of it. He tried to empty his mind of all such thoughts.

The rites were completed, one by one. He was ordered to shape the rice into balls. Do souls get hungry?

He set out the balls of rice, sprinkled sesame seeds, flowers and sandal paste over them and joined his palms in obeisance. He wound a strand of unbleached yarn around his finger, poured out oil, held up a lighted wick and offered water. He split a triangular leaf in two, twisted the halves, blew out the wicks and threw them down.

'Gather it all up.'

The Elayad picked up the kindi and walked out. Unni followed. The inangan was behind him with water in a kindi. The Elayad smeared cow dung on the courtyard and sprinkled water over it. Unni placed the rice balls on a triangular banana leaf and threw the torn halves away. He sprinkled water three times.

'Now stand back and clap your hands.'

He clapped his hands, hardly making a sound. It seemed as if the faint, isolated sound of his clapping was swallowed up by the noisy surroundings, the clamour made by those who had arrived to partake of the feast.

Achan came up, so did Chandrettan with his cold. They were followed by Kuttan Nair and an old relative who was hard of hearing. The children who were seated on the veranda looked on with interest.

'The crows never come when you want them to!' said Kuttan Nair.

Everyone was gazing at the sky and the branches. Unni was asked to clap his hands again, loudly. A crow flew down and perched on the branch of a mango tree, a second one followed suit. Everyone was relieved.

'What are they waiting for now?'

You could be certain the souls of the dead were satisfied only if the crows pecked at the rice.

Unni prayed: 'Crows, please don't eat the rice!'

Don't let these black, filthy birds be the souls of good people . . .

A crow cawed somewhere in the distance and the two that were perched on the mango tree flew away.

The faces around him grew sullen. No one said a word. The silence was suffocating.

One by one, they climbed on to the veranda. Achan instructed a small boy: 'Make sure the dogs don't get at it,' and asked Unni to come to the front veranda. He placed betel leaves, areca nuts and a four-anna coin before him and Unni realized he had forgotten to keep aside the four-anna coins he had to give the Elayad and the inangan. Achan never forgot such things.

The Elayad raised his hands and blessed Unni. The inangan blessed him as well.

Once he had washed the inangan's feet and given him food, Unni had to taste the rice prepared for the dead. As he sat down to do this, Kuttan Nair said to him, 'Just taste a little bit of it, it's part of the ritual.'

But Unni was hungry. He gathered handfuls of the rice that had hardly been cooked, mixed it with ginger-curd curry and ate till his hunger was appeased.

It was ten o'clock. They were busy laying leaves for the feast on the veranda. Unni put on his shirt and tucked his wet dhoti into a compartment of his bag. He said goodbye to Chandrettan and Sharadedathi and went down to the yard. Achan was issuing instructions to the servers.

'You're leaving, Unni?'

'I must catch my train. I'll miss it if I don't leave now.'

'It's time to eat, isn't it, Kuttan?'

'Everything is ready. The women and children can sit down inside. Outside . . .'

'I'm leaving, I have to catch this train.'

He walked on and Achan called out: 'Don't you have an umbrella?'

'The sun is not that hot.'

Kuttan Nair was ready with the question the villagers always asked: 'When will you come next?'

'For next year's anniversary.'

Unni paused uncertainly for a moment in the yard and looked attentively at the kathirkkola from which all the paddy grains had slipped down. Prosperity had once overflowed from that sheaf. He thought: the grains of paddy that had slipped down from the sheaf were years from the past and what remained hanging there was a sad reminder of all he had lost.

He went down the steps. At the gate, he turned back. The konna tree at the serpent shrine, behind the pathayappura, could not be seen from there.

I'll come again, next year.

I have no faith in all this.

But I'll come all the same, Amme . . .

11

A Birthday Remembered

Tomorrow is my birthday.

I had not remembered. I discovered it from her letter.

She had written: 'It is your birthday next Thursday. You must not eat anything in the morning until you have had a bath. It is auspicious to have a birthday on a Thursday. I am going to have offerings made at the Shiva temple: a dhara and *payasam*. Do you have a temple nearby? If there is one, you must have a bath before you go and worship there.'

My wife does everything to ensure my well-being and it is this conviction that directs my life. She has been praying for me for years. It is quite likely that her prayers will bear fruit. After all, she grew up as a darling of all the gods and goddesses.

It is a holiday tomorrow. I think it is best to keep the fact that it is my birthday to myself. If my friends find out, they will come expecting and demanding a party, and my purse will empty out. I have attended parties and dinners that many of them hosted for their birthdays.

It used to make me very happy in the old days when a birthday approached. But all I feel now is a faint sense of pain. The period poets call the springtime of life is drawing to a close.

I thought about what I would do the next day. I would sleep until nine in the morning, as I always did on holidays. Then I would have a bath. That was my goddess's command, after all! After that, treat myself to poori-masala and coffee from Ananda Bhavan. I would then throw a rupee coin on the table and order a packet of cigarettes and Rajan would ask: 'Why are you so excited? Has your wife had a baby?'

'Wouldn't I be grieving then?' I would tell him about my birthday with the preface that it should be kept a secret. I would order a special kurma for lunch. I would not let her, my wife, know that I had eaten meat on my birthday. A movie in the evening. That was it.

Rajan had not yet arrived. Had it been the beginning of the month, I could have spared the money to have a photograph of myself taken in a studio.

I drank some cold water from the earthen pot, walked to the veranda and lay down on my easy chair.

My Marwadi neighbour's five-year-old son was playing with a toy train in the courtyard opposite me. There were many thoughts crawling through my mind, and I suddenly thought of a birthday from more than twenty years earlier.

Several painful memories were associated with that birthday. More significantly, it was on that birthday that I had decided to kill a man.

The desire to kill had been extremely strong. I had to kill him somehow. Six or seven years old at that time, I had no idea how to kill in a scientific manner. Finally, I decided to adopt a new technique of murder. I would bathe, purify myself and pray fervently for his death.

I am not sure who suggested this to me. But there were these facts: among the deities in the village were some who were well known for their ability to kill. The god Ayyappa and Bhagavathi, the Mother Goddess, did not fall into this category. Gods who killed were much lower on the scale. If you called out to them and prayed, your enemy would be finished.

I prayed, with all my heart. But for some reason, my enemy did not die. It was on my birthday that I decided to kill him.

I was aware that birthdays were important days, that they had to be celebrated grandly. But I had taken it for granted that this applied only to grown-ups.

In our school, we were all given beaten rice mixed with a thin syrup of jaggery once a year. We were told that this was in celebration of the manager's birthday. At noon, there would be a feast in the manager's house, with sweet *ada prathaman,* huge pappadams and bits of banana fried and tossed in jaggery. The teachers would have lunch in the manager's house that day, all of them except Nambidi Master, the only one who would not go. It was said that he belonged to a higher caste than the manager and so he could not eat in the manager's house.

I used to think then that a birthday was even more important than Onam. We had a feast at home for Onam, but there was no ada prathaman.

The manager was an old man with grey hair. My eldest uncle also had grey hair, though he was not as old as my grandmother. He was my grandmother's son, after all! His birthday was always celebrated on a grand scale. At noon, many people would come for lunch. Rows of banana leaves would be laid in the veranda and the thekkini.

As children, we loved our feasts at home. There were five of us, including Damodaran, who came home for the summer vacations. He was stronger than us. Appu and I secretly called him an imbecile, but not openly, since he was our older uncle's son. If we played marbles and he got his marble into the second hole, we were finished—our fingers would be smashed! All of us played marbles with punna seeds, but Damodaran had glass marbles. If they hit you, the pain lasted three days.

On Uncle's birthday, we were given lunch late in the afternoon, after all those who had been invited had eaten. Only Damodaran was allowed to eat with Uncle.

Damodaran ate with Uncle on ordinary days as well. As soon as the big low wooden stool was installed in its place and a long triangular leaf laid in front of it, the rest of us had to go away. If we didn't, they would say, 'This impudent lot won't allow us to do a thing! What sort of spectacle are they waiting to see?' It was Ammayi, my aunt, who asked that.

The impudent lot were the four of us: me, Gopi, Appu and Kunhimmalu. Damodaran was not part of this group. Ammayi would call out to him in a voice that sang: 'Raamodaraa . . .'

Amma or her younger sister, my cheriamma, would say to us, 'Go and play now. We'll call you when it's time.' We were happy to obey them because they did not think of us as impudent creatures or devils. They never scolded us without reason. I forgot to add here that Ammayi had given us the title of 'rotten saplings that sprouted in an almost-ruined garden'.

I often thought: why didn't Amma catch hold of Ammayi and beat her up? For some reason, Amma was afraid of Ammayi and so was Cheriamma. Maybe it was because Ammayi was Uncle's wife. Amma and Cheriamma were afraid to even walk past the veranda after their baths if Uncle was seated there.

If Ammayi was in the pathayappura, Amma and Cheriamma would talk to each other about her in whispers. The gold thread around Ammayi's neck, on which her *elassu*-pendant hung, obviously weighed all of four sovereigns. And she had given her *kappu* bangle to be melted and remade. She was going to buy some more land . . .

Amma had no gold threads or bangles. Cheriamma had gold earrings and bangles. It was said that Appu's father made a lot of money with the shop that he ran. Maybe it was because Achan had no money that Amma did not have a gold thread.

We used to peer through the wooden bars to watch Uncle and Damodaran eat. There would be fried pappadams, a curry with ground coconut and deep-fried wafers on their leaves. I loved wafers made of long country beans. When Damodaran crunched on his wafers, my mouth would water. We had to be careful though that Ammayi did not catch us peering in.

The four of us often gathered under the mango tree in the compound. That mango tree earned more respect and love from us than my uncle did. During our vacation, we would clear the thickets under the giant tree, sweep up the rubbish and then spend all day beneath it. It was called an *urunyen* because the mangoes were very small, only as big as limes. But they were delicious.

The sun would blaze around us. If there were just the four of us, we never quarrelled. But if the children from the house north of us came along, we quarrelled incessantly. The four of us stood united against their attacks.

Waiting for a breeze to blow, we would sit watching the squirrels dart up and down, and our minds would drift to thoughts of the northern room at home: steaming hot rice, deep-fried wafers, pappadams torn in half and fried . . .

'We should have been born as Uncle's sons.' All of us agreed with Appu. When Damodaran walked up to us, belching loud and long, stroking his belly, the pleasant aroma of the vegetable curries he had eaten would strike our nostrils. Was that the odour of asafoetida? I longed to ask what flavour the wafers had. But I didn't.

Sometimes Damodaran would not eat the wafers on his leaf. He enjoyed putting them away and then eating them in front of us. I would have liked one. But I was reluctant to ask when Appu, Gopi and Kunhimmalu were around.

Once, I said softly to him, 'One for me?'

He opened his mouth wide, grimaced and exclaimed: 'You want one that much . . .'

My pride was torn to shreds.

I took my revenge by devouring the mangoes I had found lying on the ground right in front of him, enjoying his envy, determined not to give him even a morsel from them.

Damodaran was greedy. But in Ammayi's opinion, I was the greediest of us all. She even said that my jealous greed had brought on Damodaran's diarrhoea.

After ages of waiting, Amma would call out at last: 'Come on, Kunhikrishna!'

They would have served our food on the veranda. Not rice, but rice-gruel in a row of bell-metal bowls with a yellow curry to accompany it.

Resentment would rise in me when I saw the bowls. I am not sure against whom. Cursing the whole world, I would swallow the gruel.

Appu had a clever way of drinking his gruel. He would hold the bowl to his mouth and suck in all the liquid in a single gulp. When he put the bowl down, the solid part, the rice, would have formed a small island.

I used to pick a quarrel with Amma every time I drank gruel. I knew she was helpless, but I detested drinking it. It was humiliating. Gruel was served in Cheruman Chathan's hut and in the house of Mani, who swept the yard, but this was because they had no paddy. In my house, the granaries were filled with paddy. My uncle and his son Damodaran were always served rice. Why was it that only we were given gruel?

And why was Uncle so vengeful where we were concerned? Try as I might, I could not understand. I did not want him to give me shining balls to play with or fine dhotis like he gave Damodaran. But could he not refrain from scolding us? He scolded us all the time.

'You devils, why are you hovering around here?' he would shout.

We did not roam around at midnight with coals of fire in our mouths. Then how could we be devils?

If he heard the slightest sound inside the house, he would scream, 'Keep your mouths shut or I'll kick you until . . .'

We would tremble with fear.

Uncle hated everyone in the house.

'Those two black-faced demons will ruin this house!' he would curse.

At first, we had no idea who these black-faced demons were. Hearing him repeat the words over and over again, we realized he meant Amma and Cheriamma.

Uncle was not afraid of even his mother, my grandmother. My mother used to slap me if I did something wrong. Why didn't Grandmother thrash her son?

Uncle once tied Gopi to the pillar in the courtyard of the nalukettu and thrashed him with the branch of a tamarind tree. Grandmother rebuked him: 'You should not behave so despicably. You can never escape a child's curse, you know, not even if you fall at his feet.'

'Shut up, old woman,' said Uncle. 'You're at death's door and you still . . .'

Grandmother did not say a word after that.

I had assumed that birthday feasts were only for grown-ups since both the school manager and my uncle were old people. I decided that I too would have a grand celebration for my birthday when I grew old. I would invite everyone in the village.

My birthdays were never any different from other days, except for the morning bath Amma insisted I take. It was Mani from my class who told me that children had feasts on birthdays, just like adults. He had feasts on his birthday at home, and even on his sister's. But Mani told lies, and I didn't believe him.

Hadn't he once said to us, great boaster that he was, that three copper pots filled with gold were buried under the snake-shrine in his place?

But I realized that Mani had not lied when we celebrated Damodaran's birthday for the first time.

Usually, Damodaran used to be in his mother's tharavad house when his birthday came around. But that year, for the first time, his birthday fell on a day when he was staying with us.

On the day before, we were all seated under the mango tree when Damodaran said, 'D'you know, it's my birthday tomorrow.'

How did that concern us? None of us said anything.

'There will be payasam for lunch tomorrow.'

Phoo! We wanted to laugh at him. Imagine, he was trying to bluff us.

But we were taken aback the next day. They had prepared a feast! So, it was true then that feasts were prepared on children's birthdays. How come Amma did not know this?

Grandmother knew the birthdays of everyone in the village and the death anniversaries as well. She knew how to calculate them according to the stars. She made calculations to find out when my birthday would be. 'It's next Wednesday! Six whole days and twenty-five minutes to go!'

I muttered silently: 'Wait and watch, Grandmother.'

I submitted a petition to Amma. To prepare a feast on my birthday.

'You're mad, child.'

I had not thought Amma would dismiss it so casually.

I was ready to cry. 'For Damodaran's birthday—'

'You're comparing yourself to Damodaran? That's like comparing a rabbit to an elephant! Damodaran is your eldest uncle's son!'

I did not understand what she meant.

But Amma realized I was hurt. 'What can I do, son? It's your uncle who measures out paddy for us.'

That was true. Uncle doled out the paddy the household needed. All the granary keys were in his keeping. Once a week, the huge box-granary below the pathayappura was opened and he would call out in the direction of the house: 'Who is there, inside?'

If Amma did not come out at once, he would raise his voice: 'Is every one of those cursed women deaf?'

Amma would have arrived by then with a basket. Uncle would measure out three level para-measures of paddy which were meant to last the whole week. Once, when Grandmother said the quantity was not enough, he yelled: 'As if we harvest ten thousand measures here for every crop! You'd better pray that you will never have to work for your food, pounding paddy in someone else's house and being given two measures for every five you hand over!'

If there was to be a feast for my birthday, Uncle would have to give us more paddy. Why couldn't he? There was plenty in the granary.

I could not ask him. I was afraid he would thrash me, but it might work better if Amma asked. At dusk that day, after my bath, I said to Amma, 'Try asking him, Amme . . .'

'What?'

I was silent.

'What should I ask?' she repeated.

'Ask Uncle if . . .'

'You're crazy!'

My eyes filled with tears. Whatever I said, she called me crazy!

Amma glanced at my face, her eyes overflowing with tears.

'If only destiny had drawn a line of good fortune on your forehead, child.'

Amma wiped her eyes with her wet towel.

It's that fellow who should be thrashed with a branch of the tamarind tree, I thought. That wretch who had not drawn lines of good fortune on our foreheads, mine and Amma's.

Two nights and a day went by. My mind ached heavily. I spoke to no one.

Wednesday dawned. It was my birthday. I did not feel enthusiastic in the least. Please, let not Damodaran discover it's my birthday, I prayed.

It was the day paddy was to be measured out. The box-granary was opened in the morning. Uncle called out: 'Who is there?'

Amma picked up a basket and went to the pathayappura.

I sat by the termite-ridden pillar on the front veranda. If I peered out through a small door, I could watch my uncle measuring out the paddy.

He doled out three level para-measures and was about to close the door of the granary when Amma muttered softly, 'It's Kunhikrishnan's birthday today.'

My heart throbbed wildly. I had misjudged my mother. What a wonderful mother she was!

'So?'

'I had promised to make an offering of payasam in the Malamakkavu temple. If I could have three or four *nazhi*-measures more . . .'

Uncle roared in a voice like thunder: 'Who asked you to promise an offering? Those who make promises like that must carry them out themselves!'

'It was when he fell ill that I vowed . . .'

'Tell his father that. Has he ever contributed even a quarter-anna?

'It was not a marriage I wanted.'

'And when did the women here start to argue?'

'Who can I ask except you, Oppa? If it had been your child . . .'

'You cursed wretch!' There was the sound of a heavy blow. When I peered through the small door, I saw Amma fall face forward on the granary.

Hardly aware of what I was doing, I screamed.

Everyone in the house rushed to the door, took a quick look and went back. Grandmother called out a prayer loudly: 'Narayana, Narayana.'

A while later, Amma picked up the basket and came down the steps of the pathayappura. Tears were cascading down her cheeks and there was blood over her left eyebrow.

I did not have a bath on that birthday, nor did Amma insist I have one.

Twenty birthdays have gone by since then. Amma, my uncle, Grandmother: none of them are with us any more.

But as I sit here, staring out while the darkness gathers slowly outside, I remember:

It is my birthday tomorrow!

12

In Your Memory

20 September 1954.

After twelve years, I suddenly thought of Leela today. When I say Leela, you might think . . . but let me tell you in advance, so that you do not misunderstand, Leela is my sister.

There are very few people in this world who know this fact.

The reason I thought of Leela was because I found the rubber owl at the bottom of my box. I looked through its contents today, the box in which I had put away abandoned shirts, dhotis and old papers and I came upon the rubber owl. Its colour had faded and it no longer looked attractive. Only its glass eyes had not lost their gleam.

At one time, it had been my most cherished companion. I had been proud of being its owner. I had coveted it deeply before I acquired it. When I arrived at school with the owl tucked away in my bag, I somehow felt taller and bigger because I owned such a valuable possession. My owl was so much better than Appukuttan's crystal box or the Embrandiri boy's mouth organ. For it had been brought from Colombo!

The rubber owl had two special features. If you pressed a button underneath, its stomach would open up. Inside, on a tiny, soft cushion was a little dark-blue bottle. There was perfume in the bottle. When the lid was opened, the scent of jasmine would pervade the whole classroom. Whispers would be heard from the bench where the girls were seated.

'It's that boy's!'

It made me feel so proud to think that I was the boy they meant.

Nor do I regret to this day that I came to blows with Sankunni because he spoke of the perfume contemptuously as a cheap one that only Mapillas used.

The second special feature the owl had was that if you pulled the strings behind it, it would roll its eyes.

Whenever I paraded the owl before all the children in the afternoons, I would think of a story my grandmother had told us about a prince who owned a magic horse. The owl was my life. I could not bear to entrust it to anyone. After all, wasn't I the only person who understood its mechanism?

Oh yes, I had started with Leela but had forgotten to tell you that it was she who gave me the rubber owl.

I am about to pull an old page out of my past.

The days when I ran around in shabby shorts held up around my waist with string since the buttons had broken off . . . I must have been ten or eleven. Amma and my older brothers often spanked me. The general opinion was that Ammalu Amma's son, Vasu, was an impossibly naughty child. Our neighbour, Paru Amma, had circulated this notion. She usually visited our house in the afternoons and would impart bits and pieces of gossip as she picked lice from Amma's hair. I liked listening to her. She would talk about Malu Athol at the illam or about some little girl who had just come of age. I found whatever she said enjoyable. In between, she would say to me, 'Little one, bring me the betel box.'

That meant trouble. I would not bring it and Amma would order me to. I would disobey her. Amma would scold me, and I would say something impudent. A blow would fall on my back.

This was a recurring scene.

Amma was held in great respect by the women in the neighbourhood. The reason was that they could always get money or rice from her on loan. They needed to curry favour with her to borrow her jewels as well, on the occasions when they had to go somewhere for a feast.

People made comments all the time: 'That woman is sent so much money every month!'

'They say he's raking in money in Colombo.'

Achan had been in Ceylon for a long time and sent large sums of money home every month.

We were four boys. We had no sisters, something that was considered a great advantage. In Paru Amma's opinion, it was the most fortunate aspect of Amma's destiny. I think Paru Amma felt this way because she had a steadily multiplying female population in her own house. There were thirteen young girls in her joint family: five of her own and eight others.

Amma and Achan had longed to have a daughter. When Amma was pregnant again after bearing three

sons, the astrologer told her, 'This is certainly going to
be a girl.'

Everyone was happy. No ritual offering was
overlooked, no temple remained to be visited. But in the
end, a scrawny little boy came into this world, shattering
their hopes. Allow me to tell you with all due respect, I was
that unfortunate child.

A girl could have been born in my place. It was much
later that I cursed God on this account.

When I look back on those days when I was a
mischievous little boy running around in shabby shorts
with broken buttons, I do not remember much about
Achan. There were photographs of him in many of the
rooms. He had left for Ceylon when I was four and had
not come home after that.

If I spoke of this, my brothers would tease me, and
I would feel uncomfortable. They had lived in Ceylon
over a long period and could speak about Achan far more
authoritatively than I.

Amma and my brothers returned to Kerala while I was
still in Amma's womb. After they returned, Achan used to
come home on vacation for three or four months every year.

Amma used to spank me a lot and my brothers often
bullied me. I would think about my sad plight when I was
alone. Maybe it was all because I had been born in place
of a daughter . . .

Could it be because of his anger towards me that Achan
never came to Kerala? I would ponder over this as I lay
awake at night. And the question would suddenly slip out:
'Amma, what if I had been a girl?'

'Shut up and go to sleep.' Furious at having her sleep
disturbed, Amma would pinch my thigh.

I know Amma and Achan regretted not having a daughter. I knew they did.

To have a sister—what a good thing that would be! There were children in my class who had elder or younger sisters. I had heard Gopi's elder sister, Bhanu Chechi, covered all his books neatly for him with calendar paper. What beautiful handwriting she had! Karunakaran's elder sister had got married. It was said that the man who married her had a huge moustache and a very small watch. Karunakaran had washed the groom's feet when he and his companions entered the wedding pandal. I too had heard the *nadaswaram* music and the jubilant ululations that night.

All of it sounded good, but I did not relish the idea of washing someone's feet.

'Guess what,' whispered Karunakaran. 'D'you know what I call him—aliyan, meaning brother-in-law.'

I thought Karunakaran and Gopi were very fortunate. Conducting a wedding in one's house was a great event. A decorated pandal, bright petromax lamps, crowds of people, women thronging the inner rooms—and yes, I nearly forgot, gramophone music as well!

There was no chance whatsoever that a wedding would take place in my house. For I did not have a sister. My books were not neatly covered, nor my name written on them in an elegant hand. I would never have a brother-in-law.

If only I had a sister. Her wedding would have been far grander than the one in Karunakaran's house. If Karunakaran had seen me then . . . Anyway, a wedding in his house could not have been all that grand. He and his bragging!

I used to cover my books myself, though not very neatly. If I asked my brothers for help, they would make excuses. If I protested, they would, in accordance with the general opinion that I was irrepressibly naughty, gift me a sharp blow on my head.

Achan's letters arrived regularly and Amma would read them attentively. Then my eldest brother, Valiettan, who was in the tenth, would read them out once more and I would have to listen again.

'I trust the children are well. Please give me all the news about them when you write.'

I would listen with an eagerness I could barely control. After all, when he spoke of his children, I was included as well.

I often thought about Achan, who worked in a place that was more than three hundred miles away. My brothers had visited his office, and I paid close attention to their stories about Ceylon. Apparently, none of us would be able to follow the language spoken there. And they were dreadful. My brother Balettan told me that if they caught sight of a small child on the road, they would whip out a knife from their waist and slice off the child's head! Balettan had seen such an incident happen with his own eyes.

I was terrified. Achan lived amongst these cruel people!

'Is it only children they kill?'

'They would kill anyone for money.'

I would shudder inwardly when I heard this but tried not to show my fear outside. God! People said Achan had a lot of money.

Around that time, a telegram arrived to say that Achan was coming home.

There was a great war and fighting had broken out in the region where Achan worked. Which was why he had suddenly decided to come away. Valiettan, who read the newspaper regularly, knew everything about the war.

The atmosphere in the house was charged with excitement. Achan was coming! My father was coming! I would see him again, after six years.

'How many days does it take to get here from Colombo?' I asked.

'Three hours on a ship, then two days in a train.'

Lesson Five in my book said that a ship was a means of transport on water. I was afraid of anything that moved over water. I had often sat in a boat when we went to worship in the Bhagavathi temple across the river. I would tremble with fear as we crossed, terrified that the boat would capsize. Boats sailed on the river and ships on the sea. There were huge waves in the sea. Did ships capsize as well?

Let Achan arrive soon, please . . .

According to Amma's calculations, Achan was expected to reach home on Monday. We had class that day, but I decided not to go to school. My brothers did not go either. Amma allowed all of us to stay back.

I sat gazing at the gate until I was sleepy. Achan was not to be seen.

He arrived early the next morning. Balettan caught sight of him first from the room upstairs in the pathayappura as he was walking on the path over the field, with three coolies carrying huge suitcases following him.

As soon as Achan came up to the veranda, he gathered me in his arms.

I know this for sure: that if I ever felt exalted in front of my brothers, it was at that moment.

Their turn came next. Achan stroked each of them tenderly. Hitching up my shorts, I gazed my fill at Achan, feeling rather shy.

He was darker skinned than he appeared in the photographs. And stouter. A long shawl with an embroidered border was wound around his neck.

In the midst of all this, I suddenly noticed something: there was a little girl standing behind Achan.

A little girl with a pale, round face, wide eyes and copper-coloured curly hair that just brushed against her neck. She wore a dress of white silk patterned with large, red flowers. She was taller than me.

Achan said something to her in a language I didn't recognize. She nodded, moved slowly to the front veranda and stood there looking disoriented.

I saw eyes filled with anxiety at the door and at the windows.

The little girl was attracting more attention from everyone than my father.

The men put down the suitcases and other bits of luggage. The suitcases were enormous and among them was a leather suitcase with a pale-blue cover. When it was placed on the ground, the little girl moved it slowly to one side.

Tea arrived on the veranda. Muthassi, my maternal grandmother, came out, her frame racked by a dry, rasping cough. 'Did you come in the early morning train?'

'Yes. It was so crowded. Imagine, there was no place to even sit down in the second-class compartment!' said Achan, rubbing his eyes.

'What a terrible time it is! In the old days, people walked, even to Kashi.'

'They were all from Ceylon, people who came away after the bombing.'

From time to time, Muthassi glanced at the little girl, who stood leaning against the wall. As for the girl, she looked like some strange and wonderful creature that had surfaced for the first time from the bowels of the earth into the bright light of day.

Amma had not yet come out. I wondered if I should go and call her. Achan had come home after six years. Couldn't she come out?

A heavy, meaningful silence hung over the house. I knew what the reason for it was.

Pretending to talk only to Muthassi, Achan described the bombing at his workplace for everyone to hear. A bomb had exploded at one end of the street where Achan lived. A big textile shop had burned down entirely. Several buildings had been razed to the ground. Many people had died. Among them had been a Sinhalese friend of Achan's. It was his daughter, Leela, who was here with Achan.

Leela had no one else of her own. Her mother had died when she was a small child and her father when the bomb exploded. There was a possibility that the same area would be bombed again. The only way to save the child had been to bring her along.

I looked at the child who had neither a father nor a mother. I felt very sad. Poor thing!

She was pretty. Prettier, certainly, than the girls in my class.

Muthassi invited her inside, but she paid no attention. I went up to her and took her hand. She hissed and called out: 'Daddy . . .'

She went to Achan, pointed to Muthassi and babbled something. I did not like it at all. Not because of what she said, but the way she stood so close to Achan.

That night, there was an argument between Achan and Amma that went on for hours. Why was Amma shouting at Achan so angrily?

The ambience in the house was not the pleasant one I had hoped for. Whispers arose on all sides, none of them intended for Amma's ears. As far as I could make out, the little girl was the cause of all the trouble.

Cheriamma said to Paru Amma in a low voice, 'Can't you make out, looking at her?'

'Of course!'

'Don't let Edathi hear. I believe this is the older daughter.'

I understood more or less what it was all about. Leela was Achan's daughter!

Achan's daughter! Then she was my sister as well. So, I had been wrong all these days. I too had a sister . . .

I was convinced that this was a good thing. Then why was everyone grumbling?

I could not follow anything Leela said. And that piercing stare . . . Still, I had nothing against her. After all, she was my sister, wasn't she? Was she a younger sister or an older one? It was difficult to tell. I could find out if I asked Achan. But I could not ask him. Probably, she was younger. Once she began to understand my language, I would call her aniyathi, younger sister.

I tried to get close to my younger sister, but she kept her distance from all of us, speaking only to Achan, whom she referred to as 'Daddy'. Valiettan told me that 'Daddy' meant 'father'. Valiettan knew English.

She spent all day seated on her leather suitcase, twirling its keys endlessly around her index finger. If anyone went near the suitcase, she would hiss like a snake that had just laid eggs.

The suitcase was full of dresses made of beautiful material. When she opened it, there was the odour of mothballs. As well as some other pleasing fragrance.

I saw the rubber owl two days after she arrived. I crept up behind her when she opened the suitcase and peered in. I saw it then, among her clothes, a pretty rubber owl.

'What's that?' I could not contain my curiosity.

She screwed up her eyes and looked at me with an air of indifference.

Maybe she had not understood what I asked.

'There, that one there . . .' I pointed to it.

She took out the rubber owl. She looked at it admiringly, then glanced at me. Her thin fingers moved behind it. The owl rolled its blue eyes!

'Let me see,' I said shyly. I was afraid that if someone heard, they would tease me.

She looked at me again with that air of indifference. Then she slowly put the owl away in her case and locked it securely. I felt extremely foolish. She might be Achan's daughter, but she was an arrogant girl, that was certain. She must have realized that I was fascinated by the rubber owl. Otherwise, why did she open the suitcase every now and then, take out the rubber owl and make me covet it?

I had no desire to listen to her bragging. If I asked Achan, he would certainly buy me one like it. I could take it to class then, make it roll its eyes and open out its stomach in front of the children.

What if I asked Achan?

I was a little hesitant to approach him. Not for any particular reason. I just did not have the guts to call him 'Daddy', run up to him and climb on to his lap.

Achan did not speak very much. I used to stand at a distance and look at him as he lay in his easy chair. It was fun to see the way his glasses, with their thick frames, gleamed whenever he turned his head.

One day, I decided to muster every ounce of courage I had and ask him. I did not want to seem worthless in Leela's eyes. I edged close to Achan, and he murmured, 'Um . . .'

His glasses gleamed as he looked up.

I found it impossible to speak. Stroking my closely cropped head, he asked, 'Don't you go to school regularly?'

'Hm . . . mm.'

I did not ask him anything after that. Nor could I think of anything to say.

It didn't matter if I didn't have a rubber owl.

Why did the children in my class have to say hurtful things all the time? How quickly the whole village had got to know that Achan had come home and brought a little girl with him. Janu, my classmate, could not keep quiet about it.

'His father brought along a little girl,' she said to everyone.

'From where?' asked her companion, Nani.

'From Colombo. Do you know, my mother said this fellow's father has a Chettichi woman there and children by her . . .'

I wanted to shout, 'Phoo!', give the despicable creature a push and land a sharp blow on her cheek. But I did nothing. She had once given me some cashew nuts. Still, what she had said was awful. And that too, about my father. That in Colombo, he had a . . . *chee, chee*. It was a lie! As if it was her mother who had received the telegram. Her mother, her grandmother were all first-class liars.

I was very upset. Anxious to clear my doubts, I said to Amma as we were walking back from the bathing pond that evening, 'Amma, Janu, who's in my class, says . . .'

'Um . . .?'

'That Achan . . . Achan has a Chettichi wife and children in Colombo.'

The blow I had intended for Janu fell on my cheek instead.

'Go and ask your old man himself!'

I decided not to listen to anyone who said such things. Or ask anyone any questions.

It was the night of the sixth day after Achan arrived that it happened.

I slept in the room next to Achan's. When I went up after dinner, to go to bed, I saw Leela standing close to Achan, talking to him, her body touching his. The sharp odour of a cigar wafted out from their room.

I pretended not to see them. I had never stood that close to Achan and talked to him. I felt jealous. I told myself I was a good-for-nothing. I did not have fine clothes that exuded fragrance or a rubber owl or an attractive face. My shorts, with their broken buttons, were often shabby and dirty. Could that be why Achan never let me stand close to him?

I felt like crying. I pressed my face into the mattress and lay still.

'Vasu,' Achan called out.

'Yes?'

'Come, come here.'

I went in slowly. I did not dare look at Leela, who stood there running her fingers over his shoulder.

'Come here, son.'

Achan drew me close to him. He stroked my closely cropped head and said something to Leela. I still do not know what language that was. But I do know now the meaning of what he said, 'Daughter, this is your brother.'

I recall the words with anguish.

A hurricane hit our family that day. It had been steadily gathering force over the last six days. Achan and Amma began to quarrel. None of the others in the family intervened. The piercing sharpness, the fury of the words they exchanged grew in intensity. Achan tried his best to be calm.

'You have misunderstood . . .'

'I don't want to hear. I understand everything.'

'What did you understand?'

'Don't force me to tell you. Madhavan wrote and told me everything.'

I knew who Madhavan was. Uncle Madhavan, Amma's brother, lived close to the place where Achan worked.

After that, Achan did not argue. Amma kept hurling words at him, words that blazed with fire.

I lay with my face pressed into the mattress. My heart felt as if it would burst. I prayed desperately. *Bhagavathi, let nothing bad happen . . .*

Glasses fell down from the table and shattered in fragments.

I placed my hands tightly over my ears.

Tears streamed over my pillow.

After a while, I saw Amma go down the stairs. I heard the sounds of stifled sobbing.

When I got up the next morning, Achan and Leela were ready to leave. Their suitcases were stacked on the veranda.

'Where is Achan going?' I asked Ettan softly.

'Who knows?' said Ettan angrily.

I thought to myself sadly, what is wrong with everyone in this house?

Achan said goodbye to Muthassi first. Then to us. Ettan and Balettan dabbed at their eyes.

Achan did not seem to notice. He went down to the courtyard. He hooked his huge umbrella over his wrist and called out: 'Leela!'

'Daddy . . .'

Leela came out, ready for the journey. She wore a dress patterned with big sunflowers. A blue silk cord was knotted around her waist. She had the rubber owl in her hand.

She smiled at me as I stood leaning against the pillar in the veranda. I did not smile back. When she walked right up to me and placed the rubber owl in my hands, I froze in astonishment. Smiling again, she murmured something softly. Tossing her little umbrella, she went down to the courtyard.

They walked out, past the gate, Achan in front, Leela following behind. Through the long lane, into the distance. Were they really leaving?

The sunflowers and the blue silk cord faded gradually from sight.

After twelve years, I suddenly thought of Leela today: 'My beloved sister, from miles away, I send you my blessings. And write this, in your memory.'

13

Firecrackers

Another Vishu is here, the first day of the Malayalam New Year.

Volleys of firecrackers burst from all the neighbouring houses very early in the morning, disturbing the cool air. I sit lazily in my easy chair, smoking a bidi and think: when did I last go home to my village for Vishu?

It must have been three or four years ago. I had sanctioned leave this year, but I did not go. In the old days, I used to be very fond of the countryside where I had been born and where I grew up. Now, I hated going there. I found myself reluctant to enter the house that stood like a lifeless memory of hoary tradition. Its emptiness pained me. There was no longer anyone there who looked forward eagerly to my arrival.

I could not help but think of my beloved mother who had passed away. She is at rest now in the burning ground behind the serpent shrine. Countless generations sleep there. It frightens me to look at the place, overgrown with grass and thickets.

The konna tree stood next to the burning ground. When I was growing up, I used to wonder how that tree, with its bright-yellow flowers, had become the guardian of the burning ground.

Amma had issued a strict injunction: children were not allowed to climb the konna tree since the burning ground was next to it. Ayyappan would pluck the flowers we needed from it for the Vishukkani, the first ritual on Vishu day, at dusk the evening before.

Today was Vishu.

What was the first thing I had seen on Vishu morning? After all, whatever I had seen first, the Vishukkani would be an augury for the whole year. I must have seen Thankappan, who usually came to sweep my room. No, no, at the instant I opened my eyes that morning, Rosy had pushed the door open, and it was her head that I had glimpsed. The wretch! Rosy was my neighbour's filthy dog.

What had I seen the year before? I wanted to check if whatever had been predicted for that year had really happened. But I could not remember. Let's see . . . It was the boy from the tea shop who used to come and knock at the door with aappams.

'Saar!' Someone was calling out to me. It was Balakrishnan. An intelligent boy of eight. He spent all day wandering down the streets until his mother came back from work. Now that he had become my friend, he had the additional job of buying me bidis and tea.

'What is it?'

'I want four annas, Saar.'

Usually, he did not ask for more than half an anna.

'What do you need four annas for?'

'I need it, Saar.'

'What for?'

'To buy something.'

'What thing?

'Firecrackers—the ones that explode with a huge sound, sparklers and a Bengal light. Four annas for the lot.'

I wondered: did I have four annas?

'Will you give it to me, Saar?'

He realized I was hesitating, 'Three annas would be enough too.'

'How?'

'I already have an anna.'

He took a half-anna coin out of each of his ears.

'Where did you get that from?'

'I took it out of Amma's box without her seeing.'

'Smart boy!'

I went through my pockets, my purse and my almirah thoroughly and scraped together four annas. I could not risk displeasing Balakrishnan.

He was happy when he got the money. I did not let him go until he had vowed that he would put the one anna back in his mother's box. Balakrishnan had deep faith in vows.

In the old days, you could buy quite a lot of firecrackers for four annas. You would even have some Chinese crackers left over the day after Vishu. The problem in those days was to somehow procure four annas. It was not surprising that children thought of stealing money. Balakrishnan had stolen an anna. And I? When I thought of that story, I was amused. I had actually stolen a quarter-rupee!

It was very long ago. A theft committed in the days when I ran around in red shorts held up tightly on my waist with string, my chest covered with the scald-marks left by the sap of the cashew fruits I had sucked, my nose perpetually running . . .

Balakrishnan had stolen money from his mother. She did not have a steady job and was now working in the area where the road was being tarred. The image of burning hot, melted tar came to my mind. It had a piercing smell. She earned a wage of twelve annas a day. He must have stolen from those meagre wages. I had acted more courageously when I stole, planned the theft more scientifically. For I had stolen money meant for Bhagavathi, the Mother Goddess.

Kuttan, the boy next door, always had lots of firecrackers. His elder brother would come home on vacation as Vishu approached and would buy a pile of the best crackers in the Calicut bazaar on his way home. You would not believe how arrogant Kuttan became as Vishu drew nearer.

Thekkethil Appu's father gave him money to buy firecrackers. People said his father was inordinately fond of Appu because he was his only son.

All the other children I knew were able to buy firecrackers at least on the day of Vishu. They received money as soon as they opened their eyes to look at the Vishukkani, the first vision of the day.

I did not have an elder brother who worked in Calicut. Nor was I my father's only son. Nor did I receive any money as a gift on the morning of Vishu.

Children generally received money for Vishu from their father or from an uncle. Achan was never at home at that time of the year. As for uncles, I had two of them, but they were not the kind who taught their nephews or nieces bad habits. Besides, each of them had his own children, who lived in his wife's house, to give gifts to.

If only a visitor would turn up on Vishu day! If only someone would give me money as a Vishu gift once in my life . . . Each year would be filled with hope as Vishu approached.

I have seen around twenty-five Vishus by now but have never received gift-money from anyone so far. This no longer hurts. I even think I take a certain pride in it.

I used to sit hunched up in my house feeling envious and sad when my companions let off firecrackers. I would have been embarrassed if they saw me. How dreadful that I was so deprived!

If I were to ask Amma for money, she would not give me any. If I were to persist, fireworks were sure to explode on my back! 'This mother of mine does not like me at all,' I would say to myself sorrowfully a hundred times.

Only now do I realize how many problems Amma faced as each Vishu came by.

One year, I discovered a way to burst firecrackers without spending money on buying them. Thupran gave me the idea. He looked after our cows. At that time, he was my closest friend. I was pleasant enough to Appu and Kuttan, but I secretly hated them.

I hunted in the kitchen for an old key and a long nail and gave them to Thupran, together with a box of boat-mark matches. He showed me how to make firecrackers that would explode. I mastered the technique quickly. When I burst the firecracker behind the cowshed, I heard a group of boys hooting with laughter from the other side of the fence. I discovered they were the neighbouring children. I could not bear it, the laughter of those arrogant kids who possessed all kinds of firecrackers! If only I had a sharp knife, I mourned. Taking accurate aim, I hurled the old key at Appu and ran to take refuge in the house, feeling more sad than angry.

If only I could get a box of firecrackers! As Vishu approached the following year, my longing grew. I decided I would not rest until I got myself some firecrackers.

If Achan came for Vishu, I would be saved. However, his letters did not mention even a possibility that he might come. *Oh God, let Achan feel he must come home.* I prayed to Bhagavathi with all my heart. But there were no signs of his arrival. Maybe the Devi did not answer children's prayers.

'Will Uncle Kutty come for Vishu, Amma?' I asked.

'Which Uncle Kutty?'

'Remember, the one who came last year?'

'Why should he come every year?'

'Then who else will come?'

Amma glared at me balefully. 'Get out and don't talk rubbish.'

If I asked her any more questions, I would certainly pay for it.

Vishu was coming closer. There were only four days to go. Kuttan's elder brother would arrive from Calicut the following day. And Appu's new brother-in-law was going to buy him firecrackers.

There were absolutely no signs of a brother-in-law arriving in my house.

I heard that piles of crackers had arrived in Bappu's shop. A few had started to burst from houses nearby where there were children. Cheap explosives were being made even in the field in which paddy seeds were transplanted, the one where the cowherds used to gather.

Mine was the only house where there was no noise, no activity. I wondered, didn't Amma feel ashamed of this at all?

When he came back from the market, Thupran described samples of the crackers he had seen there. He said there were several new models. Chinese crackers, wheels that spun, crackers that soared to a height of two adults before they burst . . . God, how many kinds there were!

'Don't they all cost a lot, Thupra?'

'So what, if they do?'

'What about the noisy firecrackers?'

'What a loud sound they make! There's lightning in them as well. When they burst, your eyes are dazzled . . .'

'How much do they cost?'

'D'you want them? I can get them for you.'

'How much do they cost?'

'Three for three-quarters of an anna.'

'And the sparklers?'

'An anna each. They have some for two quarter-annas each, but they're no good, Cheriambra.'

I thought to myself, if only I had four annas.

'Don't you want to buy any, Cheriambra?'

I grunted non-committally.

'The children at Vadakkethu have bought a whole lot.'

I bowed my head to show how helpless I was. 'I don't have any money.'

'Ask your mother.'

'She won't give me any.'

Thupran understood my plight perfectly. He was the only person who sympathized with my situation.

'Isn't your father coming?'

'No.'

'Then you must . . .' Thupran told me what stratagem to use. I had to find out where Amma kept her money and take out four annas stealthily, without anyone knowing.

I was ready to do this and more for the firecrackers. I found out Amma stored her money in her letterbox, but the key was always tied to the end of her dhoti. How could I get hold of it?'

I looked inside all the vessels arranged under the bed and in the tin box that held mustard seeds. I had sometimes seen three-quarter anna coins and one anna coins lying inside them. But there was nothing in any of them now. And I never saw the letterbox lying open.

I couldn't sleep that night. I thought until my head exploded. I could not let myself be disgraced as I had been the previous year. I had to be able to hold my head up in front of Appu and Kuttan. I did not want to listen to boasts about an elder brother who worked and earned money. And I did not think much of anyone who was his father's only son. Nor did I have any regrets about not having a brother-in-law. I had to find a way to burst firecrackers without turning to people like these for help. I had to somehow procure four annas by the next day.

I wondered where else money might be kept in the house. And then I remembered the money-box in the machu.

Bhagavathi, the goddess of the Kodikunnath temple, resided in the machu. She had come to stay there a very, very long time ago, in the days when my great-grandmother was a little girl wearing a bright-red *konakam*. Bhagavathi was our family deity, and it has been said that our family fortunes improved after she installed herself in the machu.

You could not enter the machu unless you had taken a bath. We would pay obeisance to Bhagavathi before leaving the house. Even one-and-a-half-year-old Nalini knew that 'Thambatti', as the Goddess was called, lived in the machu. Whenever Appukutta Panikker came to perform a *prasnam*, the astrological ritual conducted with cowries, he never failed to say a few words about Mars, the spirit who lived in the fourth astrological house.

There was no idol in the machu, nor a sword to represent the Goddess. It was a room filled with darkness. But everyone stood before it with deep devotion and respect. Bhagavathi's treasure and the spirits that guarded it were inside. No human being could touch the treasure.

Every time Muthassi narrated the old legend, I would feel goosebumps rising all over me. She herself knew the story only through hearsay. One dark and rainy night when there was a hurricane, while Muthassi's grandmother and her granddaughter sat inside the house, paralysed with fear, someone knocked on the door. They asked, 'Who is it?' and the answer was, 'Do not be afraid.' They opened the door, but no one was there! The next second, the door of the machu, which had been lying closed, creaked open. 'Do not fear, children, this is me,' said a voice. That night, Muthassi's grandmother had a dream. Devi the goddess came to her in her dream, wearing red silk and carrying a sword, and told her that she would reside in the machu thereafter.

Muthassi loved to narrate this story at least once a day to someone.

The money-box was placed at the spot where the door opened into the machu. It was just an old box that stored asafoetida. It had no lock. A small slit had been made on its lid. Every Tuesday, Muthassi slipped a quarter-anna through this slit. The others in the house slipped in money on festival days. On the day of the annual *kuruthi* puja that was conducted in the Bhagavathi temple, all the coins in the box were taken out to make an offering to the temple.

It was easy enough to take out money from the machu. I wondered at first whether Bhagavathi would be displeased if I took money from there. After thinking it over, I felt there was no reason for her to be displeased. After all, so long as her treasure stayed untouched inside the machu, how could some small coins matter? Treasure meant gold and silver. I wondered how many gold nuggets there were in the machu. My neighbour Radha had told me that a droplet of gold as big as a mustard seed cost all of four annas. How tiny a mustard seed was! Even the gold dust that flaked off a nugget would be ample for my needs.

If I took Amma's money, I was sure to get into trouble. If they found out, I would be proved a thief. It was better to take Bhagavathi's money. Bhagavathi would not bother to thrash the skin off my bottom with a tamarind branch. Just a matter of four annas! Bhagavathi had gold nuggets of her own, so all she would say was, 'Let it go!'

I decided to take the money. I had already thought of the best moment to take it. Dusk. Amma had gone with Oppol to have a bath in the illam pond. Muthassi was seated at the northern end of the veranda, teaching my cousins Ravi and Vilasini a song. It was a good moment.

I opened the door of the machu, joined my palms to make an obeisance, then made a mark on my forehead with the vibhuti. I crept in, soft-footed as a cat, and opened the box very quietly. I saw the coins that lay in it by the glow of the brass oil lamp. Most of them were three-quarter anna coins. There were a few anna coins as well. A shining white quarter-rupee coin smiled at me from among them. I took out the bright little fellow, replaced the box and slipped out, full of devotion.

When Thupran came the next day to untie the cows and let them out, I went up to him proudly. Taking the quarter-rupee out of my trouser pocket, I showed it to him. 'See this?'

'Where did you get it from, Cheriambra?'

'I got it, that's all.'

'Don't you want to buy crackers?'

'Yes.'

I gave him clear instructions: 'Buy the firecrackers and give them to me without anyone seeing. I will keep them hidden in the attic or someplace like that. They must be taken to the field beyond the gate, and we can burst them only there. And yes, Thupran, you too can burst one now and then. I've thought of a lie to tell Amma in case she finds out. That Kuttan gave them to me because he has plenty for himself.'

Thupran did as told. A box that had once held Eveready batteries arrived, filled with firecrackers of every kind: Chinese crackers, two sparklers and a Bengal light.

I was going to celebrate Vishu in a grand manner for the first time in my life. My excitement knew no bounds. Each time a firecracker exploded in Appu's house, I would burst one here in response. Poor fellow, he was probably thinking that Vasu was running around hunting for matchsticks and an old key, like the year before.

Having gazed my fill at the firecrackers, I told Thurpran the truth. 'You won't tell anyone, will you?'

'No, Cheriambra.'

'You're sure?'

'Sure.'

'Swear it.'

'I swear by my two eyes, I will not utter a word, not even if they chop my head off.'

I told him my secret. I had taken the money from the shrine in the machu. The stolen money was not Amma's, as Thupran had thought. It was Bhagavathi's.

Instead of congratulating me, Thupran stood there transfixed.

'It's a sin to take the Thambratti's money, Cheriambra,' he whispered.

'What sin?' I was furious.

'Thambratti's money . . .' Thupran's voice was filled with agitation and fear.

I was confused. Something had gone wrong.

I knew Thupran was more worldly wise than I.

He explained everything. 'Bhagavathi was extremely powerful. If she got angry, she would untie the devils and let them loose. Diseases such as smallpox and cholera would then sweep through the village. It was forbidden to take anything that belonged to Bhagavathi.'

Thupran told me the story of how Chathanasserry Parangodan had gone mad. Everyone in the village was terrified of Parangodan. His madness was incurable. It was said that he became insane because he stole the fowl that had been kept aside to offer as a sacrifice to Bhagavathi. Nothing that belonged to Bhagavathi could be stolen.

'How would it matter if I just took four annas, Thupran?'

'Don't speak of four annas, you cannot even take four *kashu*-coins.'

'Will everyone who takes something from her shrine go mad, Thupran?'

'I'm not sure, Cheriambra.'

I grew very frightened.

'If I had known this, I would have never bought the firecrackers,' said Thupran.

'What shall we do now?'

'What can I say? If the Goddess gets angry, we'll die a bloody death. Remember how Chathan's daughter Kunnhakki died?'

I was close to tears. I would not be able to put the four annas back in the box now. I would never have dared to do such a thing if I had known that Bhagavathi would be so furious, even if all I took was four annas. What were we to do?

I did not feel hungry when I went in to have lunch. The images of Chathanasserry Parangodan and Kunnhakki refused to go away.

What if I went mad? I would die painfully, throwing up blood. As it was, I suffered in Kunhiraman master's class because of my rather low level of intelligence.

People beat up mad men, threw stones at them. And when they died, they would cease to have any links with this world.

Bhagavathi, save me!

I sat down in an isolated spot, my eyes overflowing with tears. I castigated myself a hundred times about getting into this mess. I should never have bought the firecrackers.

I could have just thrust my fingers into my ears when Appu and Kuttan burst theirs.

In the evening, I waited at the gate for Thupran to bring the cows back. He had to find a way out for me. I could not let anyone else know.

'Thupra, tell me . . .'

'What, Cheriambra?'

'Bhagavathi will . . .' I found it hard to hold back my tears.

'Don't cry, Cheriambra.'

'What shall we do, Thupra?'

'Don't cry, there's a way.'

'What?'

Thupran thought hard.

'It would be a sin only if you burst the firecrackers. I'll throw them under the pala tree where they perform the thalapoli puja . . .'

'It won't be a sin then?'

'No.'

'Are you sure, Thupra?'

'Yes, I'm sure.'

Ah! I felt relieved. I entrusted the box with the firecrackers to Thupran and it seemed as if I had been released from a burden, as if I had escaped a grave danger. He took it from me and said as he left, 'I'll throw it away at once. You must go to the machu, acknowledge your mistake and ask forgiveness.'

As instructed, I stood in front of the machu and prayed fervently.

Bhagavathi, what I did was wrong. Please don't do anything to me.

Madness and death no longer seemed such serious problems as far as I was concerned.

That night, as I sat looking at the moonlit courtyard, trying to wipe out the event from my mind completely, I heard a volley of firecrackers exploding in rapid succession from the western side of our house.

The noise was not coming from Kuttan's or Appu's house. Thupran's hut lay in that direction, on the hill on the west. But the sounds could not be from Thupran's hut. From where could he have got firecrackers?

Meanwhile, a tumult arose from the houses of all the children who were my neighbours.

Another Vishu season was here!

14

Karkitakam[*]

Rain in the months of Mithunam and Karkitakam is like a loving mother. It bursts out when you least expect it to, when you go close, thinking it is the right moment. When thunder and lightning set in, it's not just going to school and coming back that's a problem. It's hunger as well.

After my kanji in the morning, I ate only after I got back home from school in the evening. Every month, as soon as Achan's money order arrived, I was given two annas a day for the first three or four days. After that, with no money to spend, I had nothing at noon. As I remember it, at one o'clock, a few of us would go to the back of Marar's restaurant to drink water. Marar always filled a huge idli vessel with water and placed a big bell-metal glass on top for all of us children who had not brought lunch or tea and snacks.

When the rainy season arrived, it was only hunger I experienced, never thirst.

---

[*] The lean monsoon month when food is scarce in the villages.

By the time I walked four miles and reached school, I would feel hungry. By the fourth period, hunger would blaze in me like fire. And that would be the moment when the aroma of some dish being seasoned with mustard seeds and chillies would waft in from the hotel on the other side of the wall.

When the bell rang, most children would jump over the wall into Marar's hotel. Some of them would have left their lunch boxes filled with rice there. Some others would pay and have lunch. Marar gave schoolchildren a concession. The locals paid six annas for a meal, but the children paid only five. Ranganathan, who came from Kalladathur, Shivadasan from Kuttippalam, Vilakathra Govindan and I: the four of us drank water there and left. It was said that O. Muhammed and P. Muhammad usually had tea in the tea shop at Chandapadikkal.

By the end of the afternoon, my hunger would have died down and I would no longer want anything. It was not hard to sit like a corpse until four o'clock. While going back, however, I would begin to feel hungry again. I would walk along wondering what curry there would be at home.

Govindan and I went back together. During the monsoons, we would be drenched by the time we went down the hill. No matter how we held our umbrellas, water would find its way in with the wind. Rangan sometimes had a bidi with him. Whenever he described the delight of having a puff in cold weather, I would feel greedy. But I did not have the guts to do something wrong, for I was the son of Thekkeppattu Ammalu Amma. We were told that all the villagers without exception always said, 'Although she has no money or riches, all her children are of excellent character. (It was Amma herself who told us they said so.)

After Rangan went his way, Govindan would be with me for the next two miles. He was dark-skinned and stout and wore a shirt and dhoti. I was one of the few boys at school who turned up in trousers.

Once Govindan turned home, I was left alone the rest of the way, dreaming about the bowl of kanji kept covered in the coir basket hanging in the kitchen. It was enough to make me quicken my pace.

What would the curry be? Jackfruit or plantain? If the jackfruit was from the tree behind the shed, it would be as soft as butter and quite delicious.

That day, the rain which had started in the morning did not abate even when school got over. I had had to wring out the water from the hem of my trousers before I went into the classroom. By noon, my shirt and trousers were more or less dry and I felt an ache in my stomach.

But it was no problem to walk in the rain in the evening. We thoroughly enjoyed splashing through the water.

I was completely drenched by the time I reached home. Placing my umbrella on the veranda, I threw the packet of books held together by a rubber band on the wooden ledge and went in, calling out as usual, 'Amme!'

Meenakshi edathi's voice answered: 'She's gone to Thekkethil.'

It was usually Amma who served me my meals, and I did not want Meenakshi edathi to serve me. A distant relative, she had been living with us to help Amma with the housework and although Amma supported her, Cheriamma disapproved of her thoroughly.

Amma would say, 'She's come to us because she doesn't have enough to live on in her own place, don't you see?'

'And our house is full of paddy and money, isn't it?'
Cheriamma would retort mockingly. 'That creature needs
as much as four people would eat, all for herself,' she
would add, taking care Meenakshi edathi did not hear.
Meenakshi edathi's build bore out this statement. She was
a tall, stout woman with protruding teeth. She never wore
a blouse or a bodice. When she went out, she would throw
a small towel over her shoulders.

There was a little room in the house where the
Shakteya puja was performed. Its door was always closed.
If Meenakshi edathi came anywhere near, she gave off the
same odour that emanated from this room when its door
was opened. Meenakshi edathi would say something or the
other as she set down a plate to serve my kanji and I always
dreaded that spittle would splash from her mouth on to my
plate as she spoke and so when she served, I would eat with
great reluctance.

I spread my shirt on the bamboo pole hanging in the
thekkini and heard Cheriamma chanting her prayers.
She was evidently returning after a bath. Even during the
rainy season, she bathed thrice a day. And yet she would
complain that her body was burning all the time. Her
husband's nephew had laid a curse on her, that was why
the burning would not go away.

Cheriamma took some vibhuti from the container that
hung near the eastern window, made an obeisance in front
of the machu and was about to go in to change her wet
clothes when I asked her, 'Where's Amma, Cheriamma?'

'Who knows?'

Meenakshi edathi was in the room next to the kitchen,
chopping a plantain root. Had they eaten plantain root for

lunch as well? If you cooked it dry, you had to sprinkle roasted and powdered rice over it before tossing it in oil, only then was it tasty.

I pulled up a low wooden stool, sat down and said, with a touch of annoyance, 'Serve the kanji, Meenakshi edathi.'

Meenakshi edathi continued to chop the plantain root and said, without looking up, 'The cat overturned the kanji today, child.'

I did not feel sad. Instead, I was angry enough to kill her. How casually she had said that!

'Go and play, child. I'll take out some kanji for you before I drain the rice for dinner.'

Usually, it was only during the harvest season that they dipped into the rice that was cooking for the evening meal to take out some kanji before draining the rice. Amma used to say it was a despicable practice. Cheriamma had started it for her children Chandran and Kamalam. I always refused if I was asked if I wanted some. Would I, who had an excellent character, ever do something so despicable?

After all, Amma should have an opportunity to say, 'I too have brought up two children. Let her children learn from them.'

'Where's Amma? What an hour to go roaming around!' I asked.

I could not scold Meenakshi edathi. If Amma came back, I could vent my temper on her at least.

'Your amma will be back very soon. Why don't you listen to me?'

I stood with my hand on the half-wall of the kitchen and caught sight of Muthassi. She had picked out lumps of earth from the fireplace and was powdering them along with vibhuti and some kind of tuber. If anyone caught a cold, she would get them to rub this powder into their scalp.

There was no fire in any of the three hearths. Meenakshi edathi must have realized this, for she said, 'I'll get everything ready for you in the wink of an eye, all right?'

Muthassi saw me. 'Look, girl, if there's palm jaggery, make him a glass of jaggery-water. Don't you know he hasn't had anything after the kanji he drank this morning?'

Meenakshi edathi pretended not to hear.

I went to the front veranda. Cheriamma was seated next to the pillar at the western end, with her legs stretched out, teasing out the tangles in her hair.

'Where's Chandran?' I asked.

'Both of them have gone to Perassanoor.'

Chandran and Kamalam's father's, Cheriachan's, ancestral house was in Perassanoor. Cheriachan died three years ago. When his family property had been partitioned off, he had surrendered his own share to his sisters and come to live in our house. He had died here.

'I told them to go. Let them stay there, even if it's only for four days,' Cheriamma said.

I heard Muthassi's racking cough from the northern room.

'Meenakshi!' she called out. Meenakshi did not hear her. 'If there's anyone going to the pond, there's a towel of mine to be washed.'

Cheriamma grumbled.

'Couldn't the old woman have said so earlier? She waits till everyone has finished bathing and washing their clothes. Then she can tell all the people who come and go: there's not a soul here to even wash a towel for me.'

Cheriamma intoned the last sentence in a voice that mimicked Muthassi's hoarse one.

I sat on the front steps smouldering with anger against the whole world. Just then I saw Amma walk up through the courtyard on our south. The towel on her shoulder was clean, so it was clear that she had not gone to Thekkethil. She must have gone somewhere farther.

I sat there doodling on the ground with a broomstick and did not look up. Let her say something, then I would explode.

'Couldn't you take off your wet trousers and wrap a towel around you?'

I did not say anything.

'Meenakshi!'

Amma sat down on the veranda, dangling her legs over the courtyard.

When Meenakshi edathi appeared, she asked, 'Is there any coffee powder left?'

'I shook out the last of it before putting the water on to boil this afternoon.'

Amma muttered to no one in particular, 'Nothing will go right until we stop buying things from that Mapilla's shop.'

It was just two days ago that Abdu had said when I went to his shop that we could not buy any more things on credit until the accounts were settled.

'Did Achuthan come?' Achuthan was my uncle, Amma's younger brother.

'No.'

'Um . . . as long as men get some fluid from the tea shop on credit, they're not bothered about how the house runs. Ask Kalyani from Vadakkethil to come here, Meenakshi.'

'What did Kunhathol at the illam say, Edathi?'

'She said to wait till the day after tomorrow. She'll give me something for sure.'

'That wretch is so stingy.'

'Still, she's very pleasant to me. Can you imagine her not giving me a sack of paddy when I ask!'

Meenakshi edathi stood on the threshold, goading her.

'And what do I do today? What about sending someone to Gopalettan?'

'Phoo!' Amma waved that off angrily. 'Gopalettan! Better to starve. When did people like him grow so grand? The women there think they're so superior! Weren't they washing soiled clothes at Palakkal Menon's house until yesterday?'

When Amma had calmed down, she repeated, 'Go and call Kalyani.'

Meenakshi edathi went off and I thought Amma would ask if I had had my kanji. But she paid no attention to me. Her eyes were fixed on Cheriamma, who was seated on the western veranda with her back to us, teasing out the tangles in her hair and winding the broken strands around her fingers.

'Once women start to behave like this, only ruin can follow. Every day, at the hour of dusk, she sits on the front veranda pulling out the knots in her hair and strands of hair fly all over the courtyard.'

As usual, Cheriamma pretended not to have heard her.

I waited, ready for Amma to turn on me next. She looked at me suddenly and asked if I had bathed. When I didn't answer, she lowered her voice and whispered, 'We didn't cook any lunch today, child. We didn't forget to keep aside food for you. But there will be rice for dinner after you have had your bath. Run off now!' The resentment and hunger that had been blazing inside me had already died down. I went in to look for a towel. Amma said, 'What's the use of their father struggling in some distant place . . .'

The pond where I bathed was in our neighbour's garden. It had filled completely in the mid-Edavam rains. It begun to overflow into the fields and increased in size since the earth at its sides had crumbled. The *thecchi* clump that used to be on its banks was now in the water.

I came back after my bath and went to the kitchen on the pretext of finding out where to put away the worn bit of soap. A fire was burning in the hearth. Water was boiling in the big cooking pot. Meenakshi edathi was on the kitchen veranda washing the rice, with Kalyanikutty next to her.

'What a stench this sack-rice has!' said Kalyanikutty. My heart filled with joy as Meenakshi edathi washed the rice and transferred it to a small copper vessel.

'Tonight's problem is solved,' said Meenakshi edathi, 'What about tomorrow?'

I stuck the morsel of soap, worn into the shape of a dog's tongue, in a crevice on the unplastered wall and went down into the courtyard. Rainwater puddles lay scattered. The calf-chewed cud in front of the cowshed. Its mother had died in the rains last year when she had fallen into a ditch. She had been let loose in the morning to graze. When she didn't come home, Meenakshi edathi and Uncle Achu went looking for her. They couldn't find her, so they sent for Chakkan, who knew everything about the hillside.

When he brought home the news that evening, everyone, including Muthassi, had wailed loudly. None of us had ever grieved so deeply, not even on the day Cheriamma's husband had died in the *vadikkini*.

I wandered around for quite a while, throwing stones into the banana grove behind the cowshed, then climbed up to the veranda. Amma was still there. Kanakkarayi the cheruman stood at the edge of the courtyard, his hand resting on the mouldy wall.

'We've lost this year's crop as well, Embralma. If it goes on raining like this, we'll have nothing but chaff.'

'I've forgotten the time when we cultivated enough paddy to last four full months.'

'That's how it is when times are bad.'

Kanakkarayi put on his umbrella-hat and was about to leave by the western gate when Cheriamma asked, 'Do you have betel leaves in your place, Kanakkarayi? I couldn't find anyone to send to the shop.'

I looked at Amma. It infuriated Amma to hear Cheriamma ask someone from a lower caste for betel leaves or tobacco.

Kanakkarayi examined a bundle at his waist, took out a torn betel leaf and placed it on the veranda.

'All I have is just a withered bit of soil, Embralma.'

Cheriamma picked it up and went in. I thought to myself, Cheriamma can manage without eating food but not without chewing betel. If there were no areca nuts, she would use coconut palm roots. I had seen her give away paddy at harvest time without letting Amma see, in exchange for betel leaves and tobacco.

Kalyanikutty came out and sat down beside Amma.

'How much did you get, girl?'

'Three nazhis.'

'How will people who live off daily rations have anything to spare?'

'Why don't you send someone to Kothelangattu, Malu edathi? I heard they bought four sacks of rice for money to be paid later.'

'They'll give us some if we ask. And then proclaim it to the whole world the next day. Even if my children starve, I want them to be able to hold up their heads before everyone.'

Amma started as usual on her figures. Achan sent forty rupees a month. Most months, Ettan sent ten rupees.

'I get exactly fifty rupees on the first of every month. I have to feed all these wretches on that.'

The 'wretches' Amma spoke of included Uncle Achu, Cheriamma and her children, and Meenakshi edathi.

'Didn't the children from across the river come this year?'

She meant Uncle Achu's children, who lived on the other bank of the river. They made frequent visits to our house in the month of Karkitakam. They would stay about a week each time and as they left, Muthassi would invite them to come back soon, in a day or two.

Muthassi often spoke of how difficult things were for Uncle Achu's children. Cheriamma would scold her as soon as she began to speak. 'No one can ever be so partial as this old woman . . . she's always going on about the problems those children have, the ones who live across the river. I also have two children, don't I? Edathi has a twelve-year-old son. Does she ever call them to her or talk to them? No, no! But when those children come here, the old woman has no rheumatic aches or pains, no wheezing. She spends all her time giving them baths, washing their clothes, putting them to bed.'

What Cheriamma said was not completely true. Muthassi always called me to her if I caught a cold and sneezed. She would rub the powder she stored in an earthenware pot into my scalp and instruct me to place my finger against my nose and breathe deeply.

Amma would rebuke Cheriamma: 'At least we harvest a nazhi of grain from time to time. Don't you know those people have to buy rice three hundred and fifty days a year?'

Chandran and Kamalam visited Perassanur very often in Karkitakam. And Uncle Achu's children came here. But I had to stay here all the time. Achan's house in Andathode was too far away. You had to travel twenty-five miles by bus and then go by boat. We went there only when he came home. Not that Amma liked to go there even then. Amma did not like Achamma, Achan's mother. Evidently, Achamma complained to several people that Achan was so busy looking after his wife's family, he neglected his own mother and her household affairs.

Kalyanikutty began to recount bits and pieces of village gossip. Amma ordered her to sweep the dust off the yard.

Kalyanikutty looked very pretty when she tucked the end of her dhoti into her waist and swept the yard. Her hair, the ends of which were tied into a knot, would fall over her shoulder and almost trail on the ground and her red glass bangles would tinkle.

But it was only three years later that I realized Kalyanikutty was beautiful.

As I sat there, leaning against the pillar, trying to calculate how long it would take for the rice to cook and listening to the tinkle of glass bangles, Kalyanikutty suddenly stopped sweeping, looked towards the gate and said, 'Who's that, Malu edathi? I think he's coming here.'

I looked in that direction. Yes, he was coming here, someone wearing a shirt. Amma moved over to peer at him.

When he entered through the gate and climbed to the top of the front steps, I knew who it was.

'Amma, it's Sankunni ettan.'

'Which Sankunni ettan?'

'Sankunni ettan from Andathode.'

'Oh my God!' said Amma. Sounding agitated, she told Kalyanikutty, 'Run to the kitchen and ask them to drain whatever rice there is.'

Sankunni ettan smiled, showing his big, rotten teeth. He folded his umbrella and asked in his womanish voice, 'So, do you recognize me, Ammayi?'

'Sankunni! Such a rare visitor! Come in. Unni, bring him a kindi of water.'

'I'll get it myself.'

Just as well, I thought, as Sankunni ettan went to the end of the veranda and washed his feet with the water kept there. Imagine me, studying in the seventh class in school, bringing him water to wash his feet!

'Spread out the grass mat for him, Unni.'

'I can sit right here, Ammayi.'

'No, no. There are rules and customs for all that, aren't there?'

Sankunni ettan hung his old umbrella with the bamboo handle on the rafter and sat down on the wooden ledge of the veranda.

'Are you coming from Andathode?'

'Yes.'

'Anything the matter?'

'Oh, no, I've been wanting to come and see you and the children for a long time, Ammayi. I couldn't manage to come earlier. '

'Yes, that's how it should be.'

Amma asked for news of Achamma and Achan's sisters. And about everyone in Sankunni ettan's house.

'Which class is Unni in now?'

I said without looking at his face, 'The seventh.'

I had never liked looking him in the face. His face was pock-marked. He grinned all the time, for no reason, displaying his rotten, disgusting teeth. He was a distant nephew of Achan's. We used to meet him when we went with Achan to his house, that was all. He made an appearance there only when Achan or his younger brother were home on leave. Achan's sisters—Ammini oppu and Lakshmi oppu—used to remark in his hearing, 'He hangs around whenever you come, Ettan. After that, he doesn't bother about us at all.'

He performed small tasks such as pounding rice, drawing water from the well and buying provisions from the bazaar.

I slipped into the house. Meenakshi edathi was draining the rice. Kalyanikutty had left.

'Who's come, Unni?'

'Sankunni ettan. You know, the one from Andathode.'

'I ran around to hundreds of places to ask for three nazhis of rice. And now a visitor turns up to be fed!'

Meenakshi edathi had spoken loudly. Amma heard her and came in angrily, 'Shut your mouth, wretch! We don't have to let everyone know how hard up we are.'

Meenakshi edathi straightened the cooking pot and tossed the rice grains stuck on the lid back into it.

'So what if it's only Sankunni, he's a male member of the family who's come from Andathode. He'll go back and tell hundreds of people how he visited his aunt's house. You're a heartless creature. I tell you, we must be courteous to anyone who comes from Andathode, even if he's a low-caste Paraya. I have to maintain my dignity when I visit them.'

Meenakshi edathi of the long tongue kept quiet.

Amma always scolded everyone, including Uncle Achu. No one found fault with her, since it was Achan who had cleared all the debts after the family property was divided. These wretches survived because Achan sent money regularly.

'Unni, go and get an anna's worth of pappadams from the Chettichi's house. Tell them I'll send the money tomorrow. On your way, ask Kanakkarayi's boy to come here quickly. And when he comes, Meenakshi, get him to pluck a good, mature coconut. We'll make a ground coconut curry. How can we serve a person who's come from Andathode just a curry made with plantain root! Ask them at Kalyani's to give us a drop of coconut oil.'

As Amma was going back to the veranda after issuing all these commands and instructions, she turned and warned Meenakshi, 'Don't break the pappadams into bits. Fry them whole, or it will reflect badly on us.'

I stood looking at the drained rice in the cooking pot and the vessel below, full of pale yellow, steaming hot kanji from which arose an unpleasant odour.

Had Meenakshi edathi forgotten that I had not had any kanji? What if I told her I was thirsty? My pride would not allow me to say I was hungry.

As I walked to the Chettichi's house, I thought, it's good that Sankunni ettan is here. There would be pappadams and ground coconut curry for dinner. I imagined the flavour of rice mixed with a little salt and the coconut oil in which pappadams had been fried. My mouth watered. I would have to coax Meenakshi edathi to give me some of that oil secretly.

As I was returning after buying the pappadams, I saw a mango lying under the tree near the fence of the Thekkethil house. I ran to pick it up, only to discover that just the skin on one side was intact, a crow had devoured everything inside.

When I got back, Sankunni ettan had taken off his shirt, folded it and kept it beneath the headrest. Amma was talking to him. She would have to wait until the rains were over to dismantle the thatched roof and lay tiles. Two jackwood trees had been set apart for the wood. 'The money we would use to thatch the house for four successive years will be enough to tile it.' Govindankutty always says that when he writes.

Obviously, Amma was thinking about Achan's house which was big and new and had a tiled roof.

'This house is not as small as it looks from outside. There's so much space inside. It's like a palace, we need to employ someone to sweep and mop the floors. That Meenakshi keeps it free of cobwebs and termites. How can I manage all of this by myself?'

Sankunni ettan grunted his agreement at regular intervals in his womanish voice.

Amma continued to talk about my elder brother's job, Achan's monthly money order, Unni's (my) remarkable intelligence, the sum she was going to spend on the feast on the day the roof was tiled and so on: she kept speaking of several things.

Outside, the sky had darkened again. Dusk had fallen early.

'Don't you want a bath, Sankunni?'

'Yes, I do.'

'Unni, ask Meenakshi to bring a towel and some vaka powder from that new earthenware pot in the granary. And get Sankunni a little sesame seed oil in a bowl. You'll find the oil in a jar in the southern room.'

Cheriamma was busy spreading a mattress on the floor of the vadikkini. She was always wanting to lie down. Evidently her body smarted as if ground chillies had been smeared all over it. Every evening, she would shake out her mattress and spread it afresh.

Muthassi's room was very dark. The jar of oil was under her cot.

'What are you looking for?'

'The oil.'

'For whom?'

Sankunni ettan is here. From Andathode.'

'From Andathode?' Muthassi's voice was full of respect. It was no small event, a visit from someone from Andathode. Anyone even remotely related to Achan was described as a person belonging to Andathode.

The lid of the oil jar was covered with a piece of cloth. Another length of cloth dipped in kerosene had been wound around the neck of the jar to prevent ants from getting into it. I lifted the jar, took it to the door where there was enough light and opened it. There was only a little oil in a corner of it.

We bought a nazhi of oil from the Mapilla oil man who came by every month. I was given a small ladleful every Sunday and told to have an oil bath. I had to smear the oil over my body without spilling a single drop. Amma did not like to use coconut oil on her hair, so she bought sesame oil. The nazhi of oil she bought was meant to last a whole month.

After I poured some oil into the small bell-metal container, I realized I had taken out too much, only the lees remained in the jar.

When I reached the veranda with the container, Amma's eyes fell on it. They were filled with reproach for the mistake I had made.

Sankunni ettan wrapped the towel Meenakshi edathi had brought him around his waist, crumpled up his dhoti and tucked it into the rafters. He began to smear the oil methodically all over his body. Even after he had oiled his hair and body generously, half the oil was left over. The anger in Amma's mind must have been directed entirely at me.

I did not expect Sankunni ettan to sprinkle the vaka powder that had been kept for him on a piece of paper into the remaining oil. He let the powder soak in the oil, then rolled it into a ball which he pressed into his palm.

Swinging his arms, he asked, 'Where's the pond, Unni?'

I'm not sure why, Amma did not tell me to show him the way. I went to the edge of the southern courtyard and pointed it out to him. 'You have to go down that way.'

Meenakshi edathi lighted a lamp and showed it to everyone so that they could make an obeisance to it.

'Unni must be very hungry,' said Amma, speaking to me and Meenakshi edathi together.

I pretended not to have heard.

'We'll eat as soon as evening is over, and it grows dark.'

Amma picked up the piece of paper in which the vaka powder had been wrapped from the courtyard, mopped up the oil that had dripped on the front steps with it and threw it away, grumbling to herself all the while: 'The cost of oil now! But we can't let visitors from Andathode say we were mean and unhelpful to them.'

Why was she saying all this to me? All I could think of was the flavour on my tongue of rice mixed with oil in which pappadams had been fried. I waited, watching slivers of darkness lurking like little dark-skinned cheruman children between the banana trees.

Sankunni ettan came back to the eastern veranda after his bath, took out his dhoti from the rafters, wrapped it around him and patted his hair in place with his hands. He handed me his wet towel.

I heard Uncle Achu coming. He belched so noisily, you could hear him from quite a distance. A digestive problem, too much acidity.

'Who . . . who is that?' asked Uncle Achu hesitantly.

'From Andathode,' said Amma.

Uncle Achu's voice grew soft suddenly. 'Who?'

'Sankunni.'

Sankunni ettan washed his feet, came up and sat down on the wooden veranda ledge.

'How come you managed to find your way here, old fellow?'

Sankunni ettan grinned and stood up.

'Sit down, old fellow, sit down.'

So, Uncle Achu too had great respect for the visitor from Andathode.

Uncle Achu's respect was for the Sankunni ettan who hung around Achan's kitchen yard picking his gums with the sliver of a broomstick and waiting hungrily for Ammini oppu to call him in to eat.

Uncle Achu belched loudly and lit a bidi. 'What's all the news from your side, old man?'

Swinging his legs, Sankunni ettan said, 'Oh, nothing much. I just thought I would come and find out how Ammayi and the children are doing.'

'I've been wanting to come that way for quite some time, will do so when my brother-in-law is here. I want to worship at Guruvayur as well.'

It grew dark very early in Karkitakam. A small kerosene lamp was lit and hung on the nail on the wall of the front veranda. The wick of the lamp in front of the machu went out and the odour of the burnt wick hung in the air for a moment.

As Amma went in, she called out to no one in particular, 'Hasn't a chimney for the big lantern come to Vappu's shop as yet, children?'

It was Friday, so I had nothing to study. Usually, I sat with my books at this hour every day. Except Friday, when I had all of Saturday and Sunday before me.

It had started to drizzle. I lay down against the wall of the western veranda. Uncle Achu was describing a fish curry he had eaten once at Andathode when he was on a visit there.

I could hardly hold my head up. I felt sleepy. A faint breeze blew, wafting a gentle wave of coolness through my body, making the hairs on it stand on end.

I heard Amma's voice again on the veranda. 'Achuthan, are you going to have a bath?'

'No, I can't. I've been having this persistent cold after the rains started. I'll just have a wash.'

'Come on then, Sankunni, have dinner.'

The wooden ledge creaked when Sankunni ettan got up.

'Where's Unni?'

'He'll eat later. He ate as soon as he came from school.'

Sankunni ettan followed the chimney lamp and Amma inside.

At that moment, I really wanted to cry.

I could hardly stand up, but I managed to. I went to the front veranda. Insects fluttered around the kerosene lamp on the wall. A winged creature that had accidentally fallen into the lamp squirmed inside the glass. I crept into the dark thekkini and hovered at its northern door like a thief. Sankunni ettan was seated on a grass mat in the kitchen with a big triangular banana leaf before him. As he started to eat, Amma said, 'We've not been getting fish, there are none in the sea after the rains set in. The curries are not very good, Sankunni.'

I went back to the front veranda. If only I could make myself think of something else, I would not feel so hungry. I thought of the festival in the Kalladathur Kavu temple. And about Rangan's rubber wire hanging from the roof in class. And about the time I had escaped Veeraraghavan master's needle-sharp pinches. Then everything went dark.

I opened my eyes to see Meenakshi edathi standing in front of me with a lamp. 'Come on, are you already asleep?'

We walked past Sankunni ettan, who was seated on the eastern veranda smoking a bidi. I heard him belch. It was not the kind of belch caused by indigestion. It was like the sound that emerged from Pandi the cow when someone filled her basket with a bundle of karuka grass.

Amma was in the kitchen, seated by the chimney lamp. I took the small stool kept against the wall and sat down on it. Meenakshi brought me a bowl. It held water drained from the smelly sack-rice.

I did not look up. Amma whispered, as if telling me a secret, 'There's no rice, child.'

Meenakshi edathi's heels made a sharp sound against the floor as she came back. She said to me, 'Tell her she should not have coaxed her nephew to eat some more. She kept forcing more and more on him. At least she could have kept a handful of rice aside after draining it, to add to his kanji water now.'

I had never heard Meenakshi edathi speak so arrogantly.

Amma bent her head and said in a low voice, 'Talk softly, Meenakshi. Don't you know I have to continue facing the Andathode people?'

I swallowed two or three mouthfuls of the kanji water drained from the sack-rice and felt like throwing up. I tried taking a bite of the salted plantain bulb. The cold kanji water refused to go down my throat. I got up and washed my hands.

I lay down as usual near Amma's mattress in the thekkini, but I could not sleep. I could hear Sankunni ettan snoring in the front veranda. Meenakshi edathi, who slept on a mat at Amma's feet, kept tossing and turning. Hunger prowled inside me like a blazing torch, like steaming vapour, like a faint ache. From time to time, I thought I would lose consciousness. Then suddenly I opened my eyes. I could hear Muthassi's racking cough and the chirping of crickets in the distance. The croaking of the frogs in the distant field grew so loud sometimes, it seemed next to my ears one moment and would then drift away.

'Are you asleep, Meenakshi?' asked Amma.

'Um . . . m . . .'

'Ameena Umma will have money. Go and ask her for two rupees in the morning. Tell her I'll pay her back when

Unni's father sends me money. When Sankunni leaves tomorrow morning, shouldn't I give him at least two rupees for his return journey?'

Meenakshi edathi said nothing.

'It seems a little mean to give him only the bus fare. We must give him tea as well, but how can we manage that, girl?'

Meenakshi edathi said nothing.

'Whether he leaves or not, I must give him a glass of tea in the morning, mustn't I? When people come from Andathode, we must show them these courtesies, mustn't we?'

Amma waited for a while, then said, 'How quickly you fall asleep, Meenakshi.'

Sankunni ettan's snores glided like a snake through the cold darkness around us.

I closed my eyes and lay on my face. Pulling one half of her big shawl over me, Amma patted me and said, 'Poor boy, he's asleep. Lord Guruvayurappa, all I want is for him to sleep soundly.'

The sound of the raindrops falling on the banana leaves transformed into a thudding of drums. I heard thousands of musical notes flowing out of the secret lairs of the black Karkitakam night. But where could I find sleep lurking amongst them?

15

The Night of the Grandmothers

Several unpleasant things kept happening in our household. Our pregnant cow, let out to graze as usual on the slope of the hill, did not return by evening. It had drizzled lightly during the day, so Amma and Cheriamma both assumed it must have sought shelter somewhere. The cow did not return the next day either and everyone grew quite worried. Chakkan was sent on the third day to search for it. He knew the hill slopes and the woods well. He was always entrusted with the task of finding the rare plants that had to be plucked in order to make certain medicinal potions and he never failed to bring back exactly what was needed. He left early morning to find out if the cow had strayed into a herd while grazing and ended up in some place nearby. He came back at sunset and hovered around the courtyard for a while without saying anything. Suspecting from his stance and expression that something unusual must have taken place, Amma went up to him.

'It's gone, dear lady, it's gone.'

There was a small stream on the southern side of Tanni hill through which a narrow trickle of water flowed. The cow had been found dead in it, its four legs raised. The place was not deep enough for the animal to have fallen in, nor was there much water in it. What amazed Chakkan was how the cow could have died.

'It's as if someone threw the cow in,' Muthassi suggested.

'Look at all the gardens around, the *mahali* disease that attacks the areca palms has not affected any part of this region except our garden.'

We generally harvested enough paddy for our subsistence from two crops. But if we needed cash, it had to come from the sale of areca nuts. So, everyone had been delighted when the areca palms bore fruit and it had been a good crop. Amma realized that the garden was not going to yield anything this time.

Then Ammu, Cheriamma's three-year-old daughter, who was always running around the place, suddenly came down with apoplexy.

'We never thought we'd get her back,' said Cheriamma.

Ammu had been born to Cheriamma after two of her babies died at childbirth. Cheriamma used to walk around with little Ammu hitched to her waist.

Eventually, Uncle Achu was requested to bring Maniyamperumbalathu Panikker, who performed a prasnam ritual with cowries to find out what the root cause of the problem might be. Detailed discussions were held. His verdict was that all these disasters were happening around us because a Bhuvaneshwari puja had not been conducted for a while.

Amma was not convinced. After all, they sent monthly offerings to the Kodikunnath temple and also made occasional special offerings for the kuruthi puja.

'That's not enough. The deity in the shrine in the house will cause no harm. But there are other thirsty beings seated in various spots here, suffering and distressed. A Bhuvaneshwari puja is the only way to protect the tharavad. How long has it been since you conducted one?' said Panikker.

'Three years,' said Amma.

Cheriamma corrected her. 'Four. It was before I gave birth to Ammu.'

As he was gathering up the cowries, Panikker said, 'So there's nothing more to do now. Let's conduct the Bhuvaneshwari puja.'

Amma began to fret and worry once the date was decided. So many people had to be invited. Besides which numerous relatives belonging to different branches of the family would turn up without being invited once they heard the news.

With Meenakshi oppu in the kitchen, there was no reason to worry about food, no matter how many people turned up. Having found her way to our house from some branch of the family that lived across the river, she had become a permanent fixture in our household. She had never married, had no children. Cooking and serving food was never a burden to her, regardless of how many people there were.

The puja needed a lot of preparation, and we needed help. Kamala oppu was our aunt's eldest daughter. She lived in Vaidyaruvalappu and had to be summoned for the puja. I was very excited to meet her. Despite never getting a formal education, she was deeply knowledgeable. She could chant the names of stars, knew all the lunar days and death anniversaries, as well as the names of the Malayalam and English months by heart.

She would never allow me to correct the pronunciation of words such as October or November.

According to Meenakshi oppu's instructions, three clusters of raw bananas were cut down a week before the puja. They had to be smoked in order to ripen. The square platforms in the field above, on which it was believed Parakutty and Kareemkutty were seated, were swept clean. 'They belong to inferior castes. If you don't propitiate them by giving them something before we begin, they'll come inside while we're conducting the puja and pollute things.'

I was allowed to participate in all the tasks. The grown-ups enjoyed talking to one another as they worked. It helped them work faster, and if I hung around, they somehow found it easier to keep talking.

It was from them I first heard the story of how our in-house deity, Mother Goddess Bhagavathi, had arrived there.

In the old days, our tharavad house was not very big. The padippura, the pathayappura which the men used, the storehouse for grain, these came up later. Only a woman and her three children lived in the house. Someone in our tharavad had adopted them, brought them here, then organized an *aandiyoottu*, a meal for all the pilgrims who were going to Pazhani. After this, he left for Pazhani himself, carrying across his shoulder a *paalkavadi*, an offering to Lord Muruga, the deity of Pazhani, of two pots of milk suspended from the two ends of a long pole. He never came back.

'There were two cows in the house. The woman used to milk them and take the milk to our temple across the river, where they would give her a pot of rice as part of the daily offering made to the deity. It was enough for the noon and night meals for her and the children.'

I had heard this story before. But I loved the detailed narrative that Kamala oppu made of the story. It would generate the same excitement as when I had first heard her tell it.

'Once, the river overflowed in the month of Karkitakam. When the woman arrived at the river bank in the morning with a small metal pot of milk, the boatman said, 'The water has risen right up to both banks of the river. The boat can't go.'

'The woman waited until evening, not sure whether the water would recede and make it possible to move the boat. When dusk fell, she told the children, "There'll be no rice from the temple today, children." She boiled the milk and gave it to them to drink. Then she put them to bed. It continued to rain. Late into the night, someone knocked on the door. She lit a little kerosene lamp, walked slowly to the door, opened it and saw a figure standing in the darkness, holding out a small *uruli,* a flat metal dish, covered with a banana leaf. "Wake up the children and give them this." The woman took the dish, which was filled with rice, went in and woke up the children. She served out the rice and took the empty pot back to the front door but found no one there.

'The next day, the rain stopped. When the woman reached the temple, she realized that the uruli she had brought back belonged to the temple.

'It was Mother Goddess who brought us the rice. And she is still with us in the shrine.'

On the day of the puja, Kamala oppu plucked all the thulasi sprigs we needed from the illlam compound and stacked them in a basket. There was a thicket on the eastern edge of the illam pond and both this thicket and the space below it were filled with thecchi flowers. Keeping carefully to the side of the thicket, Kamala oppu gathered the flowers we needed.

The puja was held in the small room next to the shrine. An Elayad, who belonged to the special caste that performed such rites, was going to conduct the puja. Ravunni, his helper, had already arranged the necessary items. The Elayad had a bath in the pond, took off his wet clothes, put on an unbleached dhoti and began to draw a sacred *padmam*, a lotus-shaped design, with coloured powder. I had a feeling I had seen this Elayad on my way to school. I stood watching with great interest as he sprinkled burnt paddy husk on the floor, took out rice flour and powdered turmeric from various little containers and started to draw the sacred padmam design. A few children who had come with the visitors kept me company. The Elayad caught sight of us as we stood at the door, then glancing at his helper, he said, 'We don't want any children here. Go and play outside.'

Kamala oppu herded us out, saying, 'Yes, drawing the sacred lotus is a very special ritual. There are various designs, and they are all meant for the Bhagavathis, the Mother Goddesses. I think this one is a *sudarshanam*, Vishnu's wheel.'

Kuttan Uncle arrived just then, to assist the Elayad.

Meenakshi edathi had finished making small sweet jaggery appams in the kitchen. Catching sight of me lurking there, she said, 'Don't hover around here. No one will be allowed to touch anything until the puja is over.'

Amma called out from the front veranda, 'Kamala . . .'

Kamala oppu went running. 'Why isn't that Parangodan here yet, girl?' she asked.

Amma looked at the gate. Cholayil muthassi, one of our grandmothers, was ambling in slowly, a huge white towel wrapped around her. My grandmother had two younger sisters: Cholayil muthassi and Kothalangat muthassi.

Amma called out to her mother inside, 'Amme, Cholayil valiamma has arrived.' My grandmother, who was seated in the northern room, leaning against the wall, must have heard her, but she said nothing. She hardly ever spoke to anyone. She even stayed away from arguments between Amma and Cheriamma.

Cholayil muthassi glanced at everyone standing in the front veranda, poured out some water from the kindi kept next to the pillar, washed her feet and went straight inside, asking Amma as she walked in, 'Hasn't Lakshmikutty come?'

'She'll come,' Amma said confidently.

We saw her enter the northern room.

Amma said, 'Kamala, go and see where that Parangodan is. Why hasn't he come?'

'I'll go in a minute, Valiamma, Kothalangat muthassi is just coming in. I think I might have to give her a hand.'

Kothalangat muthassi had arrived at the gate, enveloped in a huge shawl. Kamala oppu ran up to her as she began to climb the front steps, to hold her hand and help her up.

'Don't. I don't want anyone to hold my hand, girl.'

Muthassi came up to us. Her head shook slightly when she spoke. She was very fond of all the children. She stroked my head as she came in. She asked Amma, 'Hasn't Parutty come?' referring to one of my grandmothers.

'She's here. With Amma, in the northern room.'

Amma ushered all three grandmothers into the northern room, set out the betel box and spittoon before them, came out, called out to Cheriamma and whispered:

'If they are out of betel leaves or areca nuts or tobacco, replenish the betel box.'

Cheriamma muttered angrily, 'Almost a whole wad of betel leaves is over already. There's not a second when the old women's mouths are empty.'

Amma was furious when she saw Kamala oppu standing in the courtyard. 'Haven't you left yet, girl?'

'He's on his way, Valiamma.'

'Go and look for him, girl.'

I joined Kamala oppu as she started walking. If you crossed the lane above our house and went past the compound of the illam, where the Namboodiris lived, you entered another lane. Parangodan's house was just below. Seeing no one in his courtyard, Kamala oppu stood there uncertainly. She thought a woman was peering at us through the half-open door but was not quite sure. She called out, 'Kothamme, this is me, Kamalu. Valiamma sent me because Parangodan has not turned up.'

Parangodan came out from the back of the house.

I knew Parangodan. He came regularly to our house to pluck betel nuts. He said to Kamala oppu, 'Sit down, children. I was waiting for it to cool before pouring it into a bottle. You won't start the puja till eight or nine o'clock, will you?'

'Valiamma asked me to come and find you.'

Parangodan went in. After quite a while, he came out and gave Kamala oppu a big bottle wrapped in bamboo leaves and tied up with banana fibre.

'Hold it very carefully,' he said. Don't dash it against anything and break it.'

Kamala oppu took the bottle in her hand, cradled it against her chest and started to walk, with me accompanying her. When she reached the higher end of the illam compound, she stopped, removed the banana leaf on top of the bottle and sniffed it gently. She smiled and gave a grunt.

'What is it, Kamala oppu?'

Kamala oppu whispered, as if it was a secret: '*Tharam*.'

I did not understand what the word meant.

'Tharam means arrack, boy. A few drops of it are usually sprinkled as an offering at the puja together with a couple of flowers or thulasi leaves.'

When we got back home, some children who had come for the event were in the front veranda. Kamala oppu entered the northern veranda from outside, through the back. We saw Unnicheeri muthassi there, pacing from north to south and talking loudly at the top of her voice. Cheriamma was seated by the pillar in the veranda. Unnicheeri muthassi was saying, 'Even if you hadn't informed me or invited me, I would have got to know, and after all, this place is not that far from the banks of the river.'

Cheriamma said very softly, 'But this is not a wedding or a ritual. It's just a puja.'

Unnicheeri muthassi pushed her loosened tresses to the top of her head, wound them into a tight knot and said, 'A Bhuvaneshwari puja is for everyone, that's what it is. For everyone in the tharavad. After all, this was the original homestead that people like me went away from.'

Unnicheeri muthassi suddenly noticed Kamala oppu lurking near the banana grove, hesitating to come forward. She walked slowly towards her.

Kamala oppu stood there, feeling a bit afraid.

'What's that in your hand, girl?'

Uncle Achu hurried out from inside the house at that moment and said, 'That's one of the things needed for the puja.'

Before Unnicheeri muthassi could hold out her hand, Uncle Achu grabbed the bottle that was wrapped in a banana leaf and went back inside.

Kamala oppu whispered to me, 'D'you know what people call this aunt of ours behind her back? They've given her a title, Unnicheeri Kammal because they think she has a man's mannerisms!'

Amma came out then and said with an air of authority, 'Valiamma, wash your hands and feet and come to the northern room. All the others are there.'

Hiding her anger, Unnicheeri muthassi asked, 'Have you made an offering in the Muthassyar temple?'

Amma replied, 'Kuttan went there this morning and did everything that had to be done.'

Muthassi remembered something else: 'Have you made offerings to Parakutty and to the evil planet, *gulikan*?'

Amma said, 'We've done everything. Now come in and sit down.'

The bell was rung to mark the beginning of the puja. They had begun serving the small children their meal. Meenakshi edathi came and asked me to join them.

'It's not time for me to eat yet.'

I looked for Kamala oppu, who was running around attending to a host of tasks. I couldn't find her. I stood for a while in front of the little room where the puja was going on. A number of people were at the door. Uncle Achu and Uncle Kuttan were inside with Ravunni, to assist the Elayad. I moved towards the door of the northern room. There were four of them there, including Unnicheeri muthassi. Kamala oppu was serving them something from an earthen pot on to pieces of banana leaf. When she came out, I asked her, 'What is that?'

'Chicken. Do you want some?'

'No.'

'Have a bit with lunch. It's good for you.'

'Where's the chicken from?'

'The big rooster at Vadakkethil was killed.'

'Who killed it?'

'Meenakshi edathi, who else?'

All of us children were scared of the rooster at Vadakkethil.

If a child went there by himself, it would run behind him and peck at him. It had a name as well, Raman. I don't know if it was our aunt or one of the children who named it. I had heard that vendors had once come to the house and asked if they could buy it for five rupees, but our aunt would not sell it. I felt a bit sad when I heard it had been killed. Despite its aggression, that fowl had been such a fine-looking bird.

I heard Paru muthassi call out from the northern room, 'Achutha, Kuttan, who's out there?'

When Uncle Achu came out, Amma said softly, 'Give them each a drop, that will be enough.'

'It doesn't matter, it's just once in a way. The old women really relish it.'

I thought I would spend some more time enjoying the delightful sights the puja offered but suddenly began to feel quite ill. I wanted to throw up. I tried to cover my mouth and make a dash for the courtyard but threw up before I could get there. And then threw up again and again. Someone gripped my shoulder and stroked my back, saying,

'It's alright, it's alright.' Amma arrived by then. She felt my forehead and neck and said, 'Oh dear, the boy has fever!'

Once I stopped throwing up, I developed a headache. I recovered and had a bath three days later, after consuming several medicinal potions and tablets. Amma had been quite worried.

'Kamalu, the boy's fever hasn't come down. Take him upstairs to the southern room, let him lie down there. We'll boil some buttermilk in a little while, mix it with some rice and give it to him. Lie down now. It's okay. Sit with him, Kamalu. Do you want some water to drink?'

'No.'

'He threw up everything. It doesn't matter.'

Kamala oppu spread out my mattress in the southern room upstairs and helped me lie down. I didn't want to lie down. I kept insisting, 'I don't want to lie down. I want to see everything.'

'See what? The puja's all done,' Kamala oppu said.

I was upset and no longer listened to what my grandmothers were saying, 'Where's the Muthassyar Kavu temple, Kamala oppu?'

'You have to go quite a distance from the Kodikunnathu temple. I've never seen it. They say that jaggery-rice is given as prasadam to devotees.'

Kamala oppu sat down near my mattress with her legs crossed, maybe because she didn't want to leave me alone in the dark. 'The grandmother in the temple is just like the ones here, very hot-tempered.' She began to tell me the story of the grandmother who later became the Mother Goddess.

'Bhagavathi, the Mother Goddess, was walking along the banks of the river with her three daughters one night in the month of Vrischikam. They reached a spot where the cherumans and cherumis, people of an inferior caste, were dancing. One of the daughters, enchanted by the sight, clapped her hands gently to the rhythm of the dance and drew nearer them. Refusing to heed her mother, who kept saying, "It's getting late", she joined the group and began to dance with them. Infuriated, the mother said to her other two daughters, 'Let her stay with them. We'll leave.'

'They say that this daughter is now a deity in the Kanakkaru Kavu.

'As the mother and her daughters walked on, they came upon a temple festival where fowls were being killed and a *kalasham*, a purification ceremony, was in progress. The eldest daughter was angrier than her mother when the middle daughter stopped, attracted by the festive activities. When the middle daughter came back, the two sisters broke into a bitter fight.

'"I don't ever want to see you again," said the eldest daughter as she walked ahead. The mother tried her best to console her but did not succeed. They say that the daughter who enjoyed watching the fowls being killed is now the goddess Bhagavathi of Kodungalloor.'

As I listened to this story, I no longer felt sleepy.

'The eldest daughter is now our goddess here at Kodikunnath. No one in our domain is allowed to go and worship at Kodungalloor.'

I began to feel sleepy.

Meenakshi edathi came in with a hurricane lantern and woke me up.

'Everyone has eaten. Have a handful of rice mixed with boiled buttermilk. Or drink a little kanji.'

I went down, afraid I might throw up again. I drank the kanji they had poured into a little cup, then went to

the front veranda. There was no one there except Amma
and Cheriamma. The grandmothers were seated in a circle
talking softly to one another, occasionally laughing at
secret jokes.

Amma was relieved when I finished drinking the
kanji. 'Go and lie down. Unnicheeri valiamma is not
leaving now. Kamalu is spreading out a mattress for her
in your room.'

After Amma went inside, I crept slowly towards the
grandmothers and sat down.

Paru muthassi was saying, 'Lakshmikutty, do you
remember Kunhathol, the younger woman in the illam,
teaching us how to sing and dance?'

My grandmother answered, 'It was I who took you to
Kunhathol, do you know?'

Lakshmi muthassi said, 'I remember, Edathi. Only the
three of us are left now, isn't that so?'

'For how much longer? When will we see each other
again? Who knows?' said Paru muthassi.

The sky, which had been laden with darkness, suddenly
cleared. When Paru muthassi saw moonlight spreading
slowly over the compound, she got up and went down to
the courtyard. 'How bright the moonlight is!' She began to
clap and sing:

Onnam kunninmel
Oradi manninmel
Onnallo kanyamaar
Pala nattu

Onnam kunninmel
Oradi manninmel

Onnallo kanyamaar
Pala nattu
Poo vannu kaa vannu
Palekku paal kodu
Parvathiye

[On top of the hill,
The maidens planted
A pala tree in the earth . . .
On a foot of earth . . .]

Smiling, she said, 'Come, Lakshmikutty, come, Edathi.
Let's dance.'

How wonderful it was! Throwing their shawls on to
the veranda, Kothalangat muthassi, my grandmother and
Paru muthassi began to sing and dance together.

On top of the hill,
The maidens planted
A pala tree in the earth
The pala bore leaves,
The pala bore fruit.
Parvathy, give the pala milk

All three clapped their hands and danced. Kamala oppu
gripped my shoulder and said,

'Come and lie down. If you stay here to watch these
mad old women, your fever will grow worse.'

I went in with Kamala oppu reluctantly. She made me
lie down on the mattress in the southern room upstairs. As
she went out, she glanced at Unnicheeri muthassi, who was
curled up in a corner and said, 'Poor thing, let her sleep.

She kept saying, just one drop, just one drop and downed five or six, I think.'

Even after Kamala oppu left, I could not sleep. I got up, went into the corridor and gazed through the thick window bars at a courtyard bathed in moonlight. The three grandmothers were tracing elaborate dance steps, clapping their hands, their feet moving swiftly in rhythm. Three other grandmothers came suddenly out of a clump of banana trees and now they were six. The grandmothers who had just joined began to dance, singing some other song. All the grandmothers began to make a lot of noise, then an argument broke out among them. They pushed and pulled at each other. I heard my mother's voice, from the front veranda.

'Amme, Valiamme, don't any of you want to sleep tonight?'

When I peered out, I could no longer see the grandmothers who had come out from behind the clump of banana trees. It was only our three grandmothers who were climbing into the veranda, their heads bent as if they had committed some grave crime.

They told me later it was Kamala oppu who had led me inside and made me lie down on the mattress as I burned with fever.

16

Kanji

In the wealthy households, snacks like idlis or dosas were served for breakfast and the children would carry rice to school for lunch, in a vessel with a handle. From houses where there were many children, one of the older ones would carry rice for the rest of the siblings in a bigger vessel of the same kind.

My older brothers were studying in a school in Malamakkavu, and did not carry lunch to school at all. However, when I was admitted to the same school in the fourth class, it occurred to Amma that it was pitiful to let a small child starve all day till evening. She therefore decided to give me kanji in a vessel with a handle, with two small ladles made of jackfruit leaves inside it. My cousin Vinodini carried the vessel for me. We were the same age and she was staying with us so that she could go to our school. When we left for school in the morning, we carried a portion of the same kanji we had had for breakfast. Our vessels would sit rather shamefacedly in the little room where children left their lunch. Often, it would be the vessel belonging to the girl from the wealthy Parakulankara house, who was always dressed in a long skirt, that was placed next to mine. It contained kanji made with milk, and stains where the milk-kanji had dribbled out could be seen on it. The son of one of the maidservants who worked in her house would accompany her, carrying the vessel. I often wondered if that boy ate anything for lunch, I'm not sure he did. When the girl went back home in the evening, the boy would go with her, carrying her books and the vessel.

All the children who lived in the vicinity of the temple went home for lunch. I'd never seen the teachers eat anything. Maybe because Ettamma, my cousin's mother, had given Vinodini special instructions to take care of me, she always insisted that I help myself first to the kanji once the vessel was opened. I was not allowed to plead or argue with her since she was very conscious of her responsibility. By the time I drank half the kanji and told her I had had enough, there would be only rice grains left and no liquid at all. That was what she would eat. I once thought this way of sharing should be changed and suggested as much to her. But I don't know why, maybe because she got the share with the rice grains, she would not agree to anything else. A girl must always eat the remains of what a boy eats: she quoted. She knew these tenets well.

Mornings were for scalding hot kanji, with nothing else. It was so hot that our bodies burned with heat and perspiration after breakfast. The same kanji was served to the rest of the household at lunch along with a portion of curry made from raw bananas or stems of elephant yam. But there was a special kanji that was served to Uncle Parameshwaran when he came to stay. It was a shade of light red with a distinct aroma. Once poured into a bowl, a thick film would spread over it. This kanji was also accompanied by two to three vegetable dishes. Uncle Parameshwaran usually stayed in his wife's ancestral home or with his niece. His arrival at our house meant something untoward had occurred, and as soon as he came, Amma and Cheriamma would hasten to clean out the room upstairs for him.

Amma would be on tenterhooks until he went back after two or three weeks, by which time he would have decided to make up with whoever he had fallen out with. She was particularly worried about his meals. He was a teacher in the Malamakkavu school. After I had spent a few months in Vadakkumuri Koppan master's school, Amma moved me to this school, thinking that Uncle would keep an eye on me there.

My aunt from the house by the river and Uncle's nephews and nieces from the house on the slope of the hill would all come to our house through the garden to speak to Amma and find out why Uncle had been upset and come to stay with us. Generally, Uncle took offence only for one reason: that he had found a strand of hair in his kanji or his rice. Because of this, everyone in our house would be tense and overwrought until he finished a meal and went back to the pathayappura. Amma would insist that Cheriamma and Meenakshi edathi take special care not to let a single strand of their hair flutter. Anyone who walked around with dishevelled or uncombed hair would get a frightful scolding.

Once a year, during the period when the house was newly thatched, the serving of kanji turned into a real feast. On the first day, the old roof would be completely taken down. The next day, the process of laying the thatch would begin: three or four persons would sit down in the positions marked for them. Helpers would stand below and hurl bales of straw upwards, aiming at the exact positions they were seated in. It was such a delight to stand and watch the dexterity of their hands, the speed at which they moved. I would invent the symptoms of some illness on the day of the thatch-laying and try my best to avoid going to school. The thatch-layers would finish work by afternoon and climb down. Removing their dhotis, which would be stained with soot and cobwebs, they would wash themselves by the side of the well and get ready to have their kanji. Huge shallow bowls of kanji; a puzhukku-curry made of yam, colocasia and raw jackfruit served on squares of banana leaf; a chutney made of green chillies, slivers of coconut, cubes of jaggery: watching them enjoy their meal was a marvellous sight. When the coconut kernel was being cut into slivers for them, each of us would get a small bit from the kitchen, together with half a cube of jaggery.

Rice was served for lunch as well as dinner only in wealthy houses. Children from such families would have snacks to eat as well; if there were no snacks when they came back from school, they would be upset and demand them. I remember reading that N.V. Krishna Varier would say, 'If there are no snacks, give me at least a book to read', in the memoir written by his brother, Sankarankutty Varier.

From year to year, people who lived in these wealthy houses had enough paddy for themselves from their own fields. It did not matter even if a crop failed, there would always be enough grain stored in their granaries. Small-time farmers like us depended on the *virippu* cultivation, or the first season of cultivation, which generally did not fail. The second, the *mundaka* crop in the month of Makaram was unreliable. And fields in which the third, the *punja* season of cultivation, could be done were rare in our parts. This meant that during the months of Mithunam and Karkitakam, only paddy which had been kept apart for sowing in the next season was left in many houses and this was why we could only have kanji for lunch.

Those who lived in villages did not think of kanji as a cheap kind of food, to be despised in any way. Often, there were kanji-houses in rural areas where kanji was served free to all wayfarers, and we even had two of them in our village.

It was when we began to visit Achan's house and spend time there that we discovered that rice, a sign of prosperity, could be served twice a day. There were snacks there too, both morning and evening. The folk in that region considered it impolite to serve only tea if someone turned up unexpectedly. If nothing else was readily available, at least a couple of fried pappadams were served with the tea.

In our village, workers who cultivated the fields arrived there early morning. So did our uncles, who would organize all the arrangements for that day's work. It would be nine or ten in the morning by the time they got everything ready, gave the necessary instructions and arrived home to have their kanji. After which they would go to the gardens and then back to the fields. By the time they supervised the work there and returned home for their main afternoon kanji-meal, it would be the hour when we children had just got back from school.

Onam falls just at the time the first crop of the year has been harvested. From Uthradam day, the eve of Onam, until Chathayam day, the day after Onam, rice was served for the noon meal as well. The children at Vannery used to tell us that a feast was served in their house for a full ten days, from the day of the Atham star to the day of the Thiruvonam star. They had a way of exaggerating a bit about the prosperity of their house. No change was ever made in our afternoon meal if any of them came to visit us. We had various kinds of vegetables in our garden and Amma was very particular that two or three gravy-curries and two kinds of dry vegetable preparations be cooked for the meal at night. Amma often thought about the times when all of them were busy with harvests and threshing with the feet, when three women would be pounding paddy in the outer sheds. Different kinds of rice had to be used for kanji and rice, and a special kind of small-grain rice for the kanji that was made for those who were unwell.

Meenakshi edathi, who was from the branch of our tharavad that lived on the riverbank, had come to stay with us in order to be of help to Amma and Cheriamma. She always saved the rice left over at night, added water to it and kept it overnight—not just because there was extra rice, but because she liked to have it in the morning. After washing herself by the well, she would add some salt and green chillies to this rice and eat it with great relish. I wanted to taste a little bit as well. She would encourage me, 'Eat, it's good for you,' but Amma would overhear her and rebuke her, 'Don't give the child old rice, Meenakshi.' I longed to find out how it tasted, but I never could.

The old kanji-houses ceased to exist when tea shops began to make an appearance, so wayfarers no longer went looking for them. One summer, maybe thanks to the enthusiasm of the people of the Namboodiri illam, spiced buttermilk was made available at what was once a kanji-house. This too gradually ceased.

Meenakshi edathi did not confine her energy to kitchen tasks. She split firewood, dug circular pits around plantain trees in which she deposited ashes, cow dung and organic waste. Amma often praised her capabilities. She would bring in various vegetables that were generally not used for cooking from the garden. Tying a vegetable knife tightly to a long stick, she would use it to slice off leaves from the pumpkin and ash-gourd plants that straggled over the cowshed and make curries with them. She convinced Amma that all sorts of leaves and stems were good to make curries with. Even when she came back after having a bath in the pond at the illam, she would have a couple of colocasia stems or a *kavathu kizhangu,* a kind of tuber, in her hand.

It was Meenakshi edathi who first discovered that the bamboo thickets in the by-lanes and snake-shrines had begun to flower, and paddy had started to fall down from them. No one usually bothered about staking a claim to the land on which there were bamboo thickets, they just swept up all the paddy that had fallen beneath them. Meenakshi edathi would gather a group of young girls from the neighbourhood and manage to collect nearly ten winnowing trays of paddy from the bamboo seeds before other people crowded in with brooms and winnowing trays. Once the bamboo paddy was converted into rice, all kinds of dishes could be made with it.

'Edathi, buy jaggery for an anna, we'll make a delicious payasam,' Meenakshi edathi would say to Amma, but Amma never seemed very happy at having procured bamboo-paddy. The thought that all the bamboos that had flowered were ruined and not even four or five bamboo poles were left to build a fence worried her.

Cheriamma would argue that the rice made with bamboo grains was tasty but Meenakshi edathi would insist that *puttu* made with powdered bamboo grain was tastier. Amma would then firmly announce that it was Meenakshi edathi's prerogative to make the final decision in all kitchen matters.

When they began to cut down the palms whose leaves were used to feed elephants at Cholayil House, it was once again Meenakshi edathi who managed to acquire a huge piece and bring it home. She pounded the palm, rinsed it in water, dried it in the sun and told us, 'It's a mature palm. I'd been waiting and watching, wondering when it was going to be cut down.'

She went on to describe all the things that could be made with the edible powder made from the raw fruit of the palm. As the powder was cooked to a thick consistency, grated coconut had to be added to it. And if you sprinkled in powdered jaggery as well, there was no tastier snack you could eat. We ate thickened palm powder without any of these additional ingredients for three whole days, not even noticing that our shares of rice were dwindling.

Valiettan, my eldest brother, got married the year I joined Kumaranalloor High School. The bride was Achan's eldest niece, Madhavikutty. The wedding celebrations went on for almost five days in Punnayoorkkulam. The bride, whom I called Oppu, was brought home to Koodallur only after Achan went back to his work in Ceylon. Since we already knew Oppu well, Amma decided that there was no need for a special celebration when she was formally brought to our house.

Meenakshi edathi asked, 'Edathi, shouldn't we make a jaggery payasam at least?' I listened to this question hopefully.

Amma raised her voice, 'Keep quiet now. Hadn't I told you there would be no feast, no celebration? We are not bringing her here from some house that we don't know.'

Oppu was lying down in the room over the portico after her bath, looking at some books that Valiettan had bought long ago. Cheriamma called out from downstairs, 'Come, child, it's time for lunch. Where's Vasu?'

Two banana leaves had been laid in the dining room for Oppu and me. Looking a bit embarrassed and confused, Oppu said, 'It's too early for lunch, can't I sit with all of you later?' 'We eat very late, eat now, child,' said Meenakshi edathi. She served the two of us. There were no special dishes. Maybe to mark her entry to our house, pappadams had been fried. Oppu ate her lunch silently. So did I.

When Oppu went back upstairs, she did not continue reading, but climbed on to her bed and sat there leaning against the wall. I tried to amuse her with small talk, but she showed no interest in what I said. She stood up after a while, and I followed her as she went downstairs. She went straight to the kitchen. Amma, Cheriamma and Meenakshi edathi were seated there having their kanji.

'What is it?' Meenakshi edathi asked.

Oppu did not reply. Then she suddenly burst into tears.

'What happened?' Amma asked.

Oppu wept as she spoke to Amma, 'Ammayi, whatever food all of you eat would have been enough for me. I don't need anything special. I'm not from some unknown house, am I? If all of you have kanji, for lunch, I want kanji too.'

She went in, sobbing.

Amma sat with her head bent. Cheriamma gave Amma an annoyed look. She said, 'What the girl said was right. I had thought the same thing as I was putting the rice into water to cook. After all, we can't treat her like a guest for just a day.'

Amma turned to Cheriamma with a slightly guilty expression, then went on drinking her kanji.

17

The Wedding Shirt

Karuparambil Ammini oppu's wedding had been fixed. It was going to take place in three weeks. Our Karuparambil aunt's brother, Ramankutty Nair, came to our house to give us the news. Karuparambil was Achan's younger brother Uncle Govindan's wife's ancestral home and was near Aloor, just about three miles from our house.

The first wedding in our family was going to be Valiettan's, my eldest brother's, to Oppu. Valiettan was doing his bachelor's in teaching from Madras, and Oppu was our aunt's daughter. All of us, even the children, were expecting Valiettan's wedding to take place before Achan went back to Ceylon, but Achan left earlier than intended.

Ammini oppu was a year younger than Oppu. Her wedding had been fixed much earlier than Oppu's and when her bridegroom's family insisted it should not be unduly delayed, everyone agreed. Her fiancé was a prosperous farmer. Oppu's mother, who was my aunt, and all the others in our family, had wanted Oppu's marriage to Valiettan to be celebrated first. But when Uncle Govindan

broached the subject of Ammini oppu's wedding with
Achan before his departure to Ceylon, he agreed that it
should take place without any delay.

Amma listened to the entire discussion and all she said
was, 'Good, good.' As Cheriamma came out with tea,
Ramankutty Nair told her as well about Ammini oppu's
wedding. 'All of you must come.'

Amma had always been fond of our aunt who lived in
Karuparambil and used to take me along when she went
to their house for a visit. They were well-to-do farmers,
with a huge farm. They always invited Amma for the
thalapoli festival in the Chammini Bhagavathi temple,
but Amma would never go. It was said that after the
Thrissur Pooram festival, the most spectacular fireworks
were held at the Chammini Bhagavathi temple. My
aunt's brothers usually organized them and Ramankutty
Nair was especially enthusiastic in this regard. Amma's
visits to the Karuparambil house were like celebrations.
Kamala oppu, Ammini oppu's younger sister, was not
very sociable. Whenever we visited, my cousins, Sharada
and Sarojini, Ammini oppu's father's younger brother's
daughters, would come and wander around the farm and
the compound of the house with me.

Maybe because Amma had told them that I was a
good student, Ramankutty Nair would ask me to read
the Ramayana at dusk. Nobody bothered to check if I
made mistakes. They would all be seated inside, talking
to one another.

Uncle Govindan lived in Achan's ancestral house in
Punnayurkulam. The children went there during their
vacation, but I had never heard of Ammayi ever going
there. She had once quarrelled with Achamma. Later, she

fell out with my mother as well. Seated in the thekkini, the women kept discussing such stories endlessly. Amma was very fond of Ammini oppu and the children.

'All of you must come there well ahead of the wedding,' urged Ramankutty Nair again as he left.

Cheriamma called out to Amma from inside, 'But I thought Govindankutty's wedding was going to be held first?'

Amma did not reply to that.

I looked forward to my brother's and Oppu's wedding, which would be held in Achan's ancestral house. But I was even more excited to hear that Ammini oppu's wedding had been fixed. However, a troubling thought suddenly occurred to me: wouldn't I need smart shirt and trousers when going for the wedding? I continued to think about my clothes obsessively.

I was in the fourth class. I had three shirts and two pairs of trousers. The third shirt was meant for an emergency during the rainy season, in case a washed one had not dried. All these clothes were made of cheap material. In those days, a weaver used to come once a month from across the river, carrying a huge cloth bundle on his head. Everyone called him 'Neythan', meaning weaver. Most of the clothes he had in the bundle were large-sized dhotis and hand-woven towels. In between, there would be some lengths of cheap printed cloth. Amma would first give him some money towards materials she had bought earlier and then buy a few bits and pieces as if to keep him in good humour. He would note down the details in his little notebook. My shirts and trousers were generally made from material that she had asked him to buy at the shandy in Palathara or someplace like that. There were a few boys in our class who had no shirts to wear at all. Because of this, I never looked at anyone's clothes with a competitive eye.

As the date of the wedding drew nearer, I began to worry more and more about how to ensure I would have a new shirt to wear for the occasion. I did not have the courage to ask Amma to get me one. I mentioned it to my brother Kochunni ettan once and he spoke to Amma on my behalf. Amma said indifferently, 'There were all sorts of things in the suitcases your father brought. I saw him picking up handfuls and distributing them to people. Go and look.'

When Achan came back from Ceylon, his suitcases used to be full of lengths of cloth. Lots of people would turn up, relatives as well as neighbours, for the opening of the suitcase, an eventful moment for all. As he took out things one by one and described its good qualities, many greedy hands would stretch out. Achan would distribute everything. I had heard all these stories, but I could not remember his earlier arrivals.

One time, we were expecting his arrival and everyone at home as well as all our relatives were waiting for him impatiently. Three coolies had been sent to the Pallipuram station. Koorthuvalappil Kuttettan was busily extracting juice from mangoes plucked from the tree on the hill slope above us, since Achan had to be given something to drink as soon as he arrived. This time, he was accompanied by two or three assistants who worked with him, all of whom were related to us. Achan had got them their jobs in Ceylon. There was a little girl with them too. At first, we were told that she was the daughter of a relative who had died in a bomb blast. At dusk that day, one of the assistants whispered to someone that the girl was Achan's child. That night, there was a huge quarrel between Achan and Amma, an event I have described in the story, 'In Your Memory'.

Achan had arrived as usual in the evening. He distributed the lengths of material he had brought among those who had gathered. None of us partook in this event. And Achan went off to Punnayoorkkulam the next day.

I went with Kochunni ettan to examine the contents of the suitcases. There were two pieces of striped cloth. I asked, 'Won't these be suitable for shirts?'

Kochunni ettan said, 'This is mattress-cloth, boy, they are meant for pillowcases.'

So, the problem of my clothes for the wedding remained unsolved.

When only a week was left for the wedding, I plucked up enough courage to say to Amma, 'I have no good shirts, Amma. Won't the children who come for the wedding make fun of me?'

Amma examined all my three shirts carefully. She thought one of them was not too bad. 'What's wrong with this, boy?'

'Look at it very carefully, Amma.'

Amma was convinced it was unsuitable when she scrutinized it. I had stumbled and fallen down once when walking through the corridor at dusk. A mixture to sprinkle on areca palms to prevent the mahali disease ruining them had been stored there in a big circular vessel covered by a banana leaf. What I fell into was a solution in which copper sulphate and blue vitriol had been dissolved. Meenakshi edathi said, 'We can wash out the stains.' Although she washed it many times, the stains continued to cling here and there to the shirt.

Amma cursed the weaver. He came often enough but never brought cloth that was suitable for children. I was sure destiny had willed that I wear my faded, crumpled shirt at the wedding. I had never participated in a wedding. Tailors in Chalisserry and Kunnamkulam must now be sewing excellent shirts for children in many houses, I thought. Next day, Amma considered the problem of my shirt again and said, 'Go to Kothalangat and speak to Valiamma. Kuttan has lots of shirts and trousers that are not tailored here in Palathara. His elder brother Balan buys excellent material in Kozhikode, gets them stitched there and brings them home for him. They're not strangers to us, after all. Ask him to give you a shirt and a pair of trousers.'

The next day was a holiday. Kuttan was two years older than I, but we were of the same physical build. But he had stopped going to school because of his epileptic fits.

Whenever I went there, Valiamma would give me all kinds of things to eat. She would never allow me to refuse them, however much I protested. Kuttan was on the farm, watching the *kalathekku*, a newly installed contraption operated by bulls to water the field. I went up to him.

I noted that Kuttan wore smart shirts and trousers even when he was at home. He told me that ordinary bulls could not be used for the kalathekku and described the special qualities of the bulls that had just been bought. I managed to give him a hint about the wedding at Karuparambil. 'They came here to invite us. But they are not that close to us. None of us will be going. Achu ettan might go,' he said.

I accompanied Kuttan as he walked around the farm and the compound. All the while, I kept thinking: if the shirts and trousers he wears at home are so well-tailored, how many finer clothes there must be in his suitcase!

A little while later, Valiamma called out, 'It's time for lunch, Kuttan.

Tell Vasu he must eat before he leaves.'

The men at the kalathekku had stopped working and were untying the bulls. Kuttan asked, 'Aren't you coming? It's time for lunch.'

'I'll leave now. I didn't tell Amma I was going out.'

I went straight home. Amma asked, 'Didn't you pick up a shirt?'

I lied, 'He doesn't have anything that fits me, Amma.'

Amma searched through Achan's suitcases all day. She took out the length of cloth that Kochunni ettan had scorned as fit for pillowcases and brought it to the front veranda. With Meenakshi edathi's help, she unfolded and examined it.

'What's wrong with this, boy? It will look fine if it's made into a shirt, isn't that so, Meenakshi?'

Meenakshi edathi agreed.

'Go to the bazaar when the sun goes down. Doesn't Apputty sit and sew on a machine in front of that Mohammed's shop? Ask him to take your measurements and make two shirts for you. We need one of them at once, he can give us the other later. How could Kochunni have thought this can only be mattress-cloth?'

Scrutinizing the cloth again and again, I too felt that it was not all that bad. Would Achan have bothered to buy cloth suitable only for covering a mattress from a place so far away and bring it home? Could it be that my older brothers did not like to see me wearing a smart shirt?

That evening, I wrapped the cloth in a piece pf paper and went to the tailor. He was having a conversation with Appukuttan Nair, who had left our village a long time

ago and returned very recently. The rumour was that he
had been in some theatre group. He always had a stripe
of *sindooram,* vermilion, drawn across his forehead, and
kajal in his eyes. When people gathered at dusk, he would
sing songs from Tamil musicals. He knew me because I
often stopped to listen to him when I went to buy utilities.
As soon as he realized what I wanted, he became my
enthusiastic helper. He suggested some fashion tips while
Apputty took my measurements. He looked closely at both
sides of the cloth and remarked, 'Your father brought this,
right? It's very good cloth.'

I don't quite know why, but I felt immensely relieved.

We left for the Karuparambil wedding a day early, just
Amma and I. There were braided date palm leaves on both
sides of the path to the house. The pandal was huge and
beyond it was the dining shed, which was being supervised
by Ramankutty Nair. It was the first time I was seeing all
the preparations made for a wedding.

Amma had a look at all the jewels and clothes that
Ammini oppu was going to wear. Two young boys were
deputed to be companions to Sharada, Sarojini and me.
They were distant relatives. A wedding had taken place
recently in one of the houses and they told us proudly that
they had had 'music-in-a-box' at the function. 'We tried to
get one too, but it was not available on rent.'

On the day of the wedding, I had a bath early morning
and got ready. I felt quite calm as I put on my new shirt.
Sharada combed my hair once again and patted it in place.

Sharada and Sarojini said, 'Hai! What a nice shirt!'

I exulted. Wasn't everyone looking at me with envy?
Yes, they were! I heard the pipes and drums of the
nadaswaram at the gate. The bridegroom's retinue was

approaching. Ramankutty Nair came and inspected all of us boys briefly. He then gripped my shoulder and said, 'Come, come, you must stand over there and sprinkle rosewater on them as they enter.' He gave me the sprinkler. I sniffed it stealthily. A lovely fragrance. I stood at the spot that Ramankutty Nair had indicated and sprinkled rosewater on the bridegroom's group as they came in while the other children watched me enviously. I took no notice of them. Ramankutty Nair had entrusted me with a great responsibility. Surely, Amma would have realized this?

As we were getting ready to go back that evening, Amma said, 'Look here, boy, take off that shirt. Yesterday's will do for the return journey.'

I pretended not to have heard her. Wearing my striped shirt and clutching the lime I had been given after the wedding feast, I walked behind Amma.

18

Money

Kuttiraman counted out the cash for me during the afternoon recess. The three-quarter anna and one-anna coins he set out in front of me added up to five and a half annas. I put the coins in my trouser pocket.

'Should I wrap them up in a piece of paper?'

'No, I'll be careful with them.'

Kuttiraman was one of the children who came without a shirt to the Malamakkavil school. He was bigger than the rest of us in the fourth class. His regular attire was a large hand-woven cotton towel that extended well below his knees. He wanted a box of coloured pencils to be bought from Kumaranallur. Two of my older brothers were studying there. Kuttiraman knew that coloured pencils were available in Kandikkan's shop in Kumaranallur and he knew the exact price as well, five and a half annas. He wanted me to request one of my older brothers to buy them. Why did Kuttiraman want the coloured pencils? I didn't ask. I felt proud that I had been given this responsibility by Kuttiraman, the eldest of us. I took care not to let the coins in my pocket jingle. There were four or five children with me as we walked home from school. Two of them, daughters of an uncle who lived next door to us, were older than me. The boys were from different homes on the hill slope above our house and they usually walked ahead of us. I walked very slowly, and my uncle's daughters kept pace with me.

I had arrived in the fourth class without ever attending the first and after spending only a few months in the second. Though I was only about seven or eight, I was allowed to join the fourth class because Uncle Parameshwaran was a teacher in that school. The girls had been given the task of making sure I did not stumble and fall anywhere. We had to walk quite a distance over the Malamakkavu hill to reach Tanni hill, which was just behind our house.

I didn't tell the other children about the money Kuttiraman had entrusted to me. The western side of the Malamakkavu hill was a grazing ground and there were always cattle there, though they never strayed into our path. It looked as though there was a chance of a very light drizzle. Catching sight of a buffalo that was part of a herd grazing quite faraway bellow and suddenly veer towards us, the older of the girls said, 'Ayyo, run, it's a wild buffalo!' Everyone started to run and I followed. There was a little stream just beyond the Malamakkavu hill. Once you crossed it, you could go up our Tanni hill. We turned to look and found that, for some reason, the bellowing buffalo had run into another path. Relieved, we walked on. As we went down the hill and entered the lane, I put my hand in my pocket, only to discover that there was less money in it than there should have been. Anxiously, I took out all the coins and checked, there were

only two three-quarter annas and a two-anna coin. I was
on the verge of tears. I told the girls what had happened. I
insisted that since the coins must have fallen out when we
caught sight of the buffalo and started to run, we should
go back the way we came and search for them. It was quite
a distance, but seeing how upset I was, they consented to
go back a little way. We walked almost up to the pala tree
under which the annual thalapoli festival was always held
but did not find the money.

My older brothers would arrive the following Saturday
and return to Kumaranalloor on Sunday. I had to give them
Kuttiraman's money as soon as they came. At dusk, while
coming back after a bath in the pond at Vadakkethu, I
hung around their kitchen yard. Padmu, one of the children
at Vadakkethu, saw me and came out. I told her about the
loss and explained that it must have happened because the
girls had egged me on to run. They had to help me find the
money now. I could not tell my brothers that I had lost
it. Realizing how sad and angry I was, Padmu's younger
sister suggested that all of them would help me and make
an effort to somehow procure the four annas I had lost. It
was only when I got back home that I asked myself, where
was the money in our house kept?

Although Amma looked after the household affairs, I
had never seen her handle money. I had a vague idea it
was kept upstairs in a small wooden box with four legs.
Labourers who came back in the evening after working in
the fields were paid in kind with paddy which Uncle Kuttan
measured out for them. I used to be sent to Abdu's shop to
buy small quantities of provisions and Abdu would make a
note of whatever I bought in a notebook. Lists were made
out for larger quantities and Uncle Kuttan would go and

buy them. I think they were also noted down in the same book. Whenever anyone from our house crossed the river to go to Pallippuram or Kodikkunnath, no one paid the boatman any money. Paddy was measured out and given to him at the Onam and Vishu festivals every year, according to some account they maintained. The only occasion when Uncle Kuttan handed over a sum of money to Amma was when he came back after selling areca nuts in Chalisserry.

I had no idea whether Padmu would be able to find money anywhere. I looked everywhere for anna or three-quarter anna coins. I was scared to say anything to Amma, for she was sure to ask why I had accepted someone else's cash at all. I knew she always kept the key of the four-legged wooden box hidden in some secret place which I would never be able to find. And even if I were to find it, I would never have the guts to open the box and take out the money. When I arrived at school the following Monday, Kuttiraman asked if I had given my brothers the money and I murmured yes without looking him in the face. That evening, while going back home, Subhadra, my shoolmate, gave a yell of astonishment: there was an anna lying on the grass. We searched but found nothing more.

After two or three days, Padmu whispered to me that she had stealthily managed to take two annas for herself while handing over to Ammayi the sum of money they had received for the sale of raw bananas from their garden.

Once again, I lied to Kuttiraman. That my brothers had decided at the last moment that weekend to go to Achan's house in Punnayurkulam rather than come to Koodallur. Even as I kept grieving, remembering I needed more coins, I found an anna under the staircase. It was a surprise; I don't know from whose hand it had dropped down. Anyway, I now had the whole amount that Kuttiraman had given me and could hand it over to my brothers when they came. I did so, telling them about the box of coloured pencils for Kuttiraman. The experience taught me that money was a wondrous thing. It could jump out of one's pocket and disappear and it could also suddenly appear before one's eyes when least expected.

Although my problem had been solved for the moment, I began to watch Amma attentively whenever she counted out cash or placed it in the wooden box.

While I was in high school, it was Kochunni ettan who managed all our money transactions. Balettan had finished high school by that time and left, so Amma entrusted all her financial affairs to Kochunni ettan. Although Amma was not highly educated, she was very strict about accounts and it was very difficult to get her to part with money. We could coax her to part with small sums occasionally by telling her little white lies, but Kochunni ettan would never stoop to such wiles. We lived in a rented house and did not really need much money. If we convinced Amma that we wanted money for small things such as cutting our hair, she would give us enough.

A cinema house which showed 'talkies' had recently opened its doors in Ponnani and children who went there to watch films used to tell us about them. But we were not particularly keen on seeing them ourselves. A distant relative of ours, Gopi ettan, lived with us to help with household chores and it was he who cooked our food. Once, he prepared our meal of rice and curries well ahead of time and went to Ponnani to watch a film. The next day, he described all the comic scenes that N.S. Krishnan and T.A. Madhuram had enacted. Even after listening to him, we had no desire to go to Ponnani to watch a film.

There were certain luxuries that Amma would not allow us and getting our clothes ironed was one of them. Someone in the village had started an ironing business in the local bazaar. The shirts he ironed had a gentle fragrance. People said it was because he used some kind of special powder. Kochunni ettan thought we needed to be given money for rare requirements such as this, but Amma did not agree with him.

When Achan's nephew, Balettan, came to live with us to pursue his studies, we began to accompany him to Achan's house in Punnayoorkkulam once a month. We enjoyed these visits, for food was served there in abundance and we even had snacks twice a day. There were fried jackfruit seeds to eat. And there was a special delicacy available there that people had not yet started cultivating in our region: tapioca, known there as *mathokku*. In our region, we had only sweet potatoes.

The bus charge to go from Kumaranallur to Kunnamkulam was ten annas and you had to walk six miles from Kunnamkulam to reach Punnayoorkkulam. Balettan, who was fun-loving and lively, became a hero in school as soon as he joined. He was a good badminton player as well. Balettan discovered that it was simpler to walk the twelve or thirteen miles from Kumaranalloor to Punnayoorkkulam by way of Changaramkulam rather than spend ten annas to go by bus to Kunnamkulam and walk the remaining six miles. We would therefore bunk the last period every Friday, start walking, stop in Changaramkulam to have tea in a tea shop and reach Achan's house before dusk. In those days, Achan was in Ceylon and his younger brother, Uncle

Govindan, who was a teacher in the elementary school, looked after the arable lands and the coconut plantations.

Achan had another younger brother, Uncle Madhavan, who was a tea maker in a huge tea estate in the Nilgiris. Uncle Govindan used to buy new fields for cultivation and new coconut plantations with the money that Achan and Uncle Madhavan sent. However, all the accounts had to be submitted to Achamma. It was Achan who had the old house demolished and rebuilt, while Uncle Madhavan had a pathayappura constructed next to it.

There was a cot with springs and many beautiful artefacts in one of the rooms upstairs in this pathayappura. Although Uncle Madhavan's wife's ancestral house was only two or three miles away, he always stayed in this pathayappura whenever he came to Kerala. His wife, our Ammayi, and their children would come there to see him.

There were big wooden boxes for storing grains in the central room downstairs in the pathayappura. Achamma slept in the little space that remained on the floor. We always saw her seated on a grass mat, with her legs stretched out, running her fingers through her hair to tease out the tangles. She had poor eyesight. Uncle Govindan explained the details of all financial transactions to her while the money itself remained in her custody.

Before we returned on Sunday evening, Balettan would hover around Achamma, murmuring that he needed money for this and that, but we never saw Achamma give him any. Sometimes, she would say angrily, 'From where would I get any money?' As we were leaving, Achamma would give Kochunni ettan and me five rupees each as travelling expenses. She often handed over the money for both of us to me. Once we reached Kumaranalloor, Balettan was entitled to receive a share of this sum. Unlike us, he liked to go and have tea in a hotel after a badminton game in the evening. Once in a way, he also liked to eat chops in Balan Nair's hotel. This was a time when a single meal cost four annas and a plate of chops cost much the same. Kochunni ettan was aware of all this, but still gave Balettan his share of the money uncomplainingly.

It was not easy at all to induce Achamma to part with money. An organization called the P.C.C. Society had been started with Ponnani as headquarters, and one of its objectives was to buy paddy from those who stored large quantities of it at a price fixed by the government. Once, Balettan and Oppu (Achan's eldest niece who later became my eldest brother's wife) hatched a conspiracy together. There were several suitcases in the middle room upstairs in the pathayappura that Uncle Madhavan had brought and left behind on various occasions. One contained old Tamil magazines and there were old coats and pants in another one. Oppu and Balettan took out some of these clothes, took them to a corner of the yard and changed into them. When she caught sight of the two of them walking towards the house, Achamma was worried. Someone said to her, 'They've come to measure the paddy.' Although she would get the government price for the paddy later, Ittimayamma, our achamma, could not bear the thought of the paddy in her storage boxes being measured out and taken away. Karthiyayani Oppu came up and said, 'Tell them you don't have any paddy, give them some money and send them away.' Since her vision was poor, Achamma did not recognize her grandchildren in those old coats and pants. Cursing them, she gave them some money! Oppu herself narrated this incident to us.

The results of the SSLC examination came out in April. My certificate showed that I had secured fairly good marks, so there was a discussion on which college I should join. Meanwhile, circumstances had changed at home. In Ceylon, those who did not accept citizenship had to abide by strict restrictions if they wanted to send money abroad. Kochunni ettan was already studying in the government college in Mangalore; it would be difficult to finance two students in college at the same time. Valiettan, my eldest brother, discussed these matters with Amma. Kochunni ettan would have to stop his studies as soon as he finished the Intermediate and look for a job. Eventually, they took a decision to send me to college only after a year. Although it upset me initially, in retrospect I feel that year at home proved to be a turning point in my life.

I used to go once a week to the poet Akkitham's illam in Kumaranallur to bring back a whole bundle of books. Most of the time, Akkitham himself would not be at home. His brothers, Vasudevan and Parameswaran, were my good friends. I chose books in Malayalam as well as English. And I wrote, all day and all night. I wrote articles, poems and stories, sent off many of them to various magazines. Sending letters and packets by book post was not easy, the problem was always finding money. I did not write many letters, there was no need to. But I needed three quarters of an anna to send anything by book post. Amma's financial difficulties had begun, so it was very rarely that I asked her for a few coins.

That year, two miraculous incidents took place. I translated 'My Uncle Jule', a story by Maupassant into Malayalam and sent it to *Chandrika,* a weekly magazine and it was printed and published! Two weeks later, I received a money order for four rupees and fourteen annas, from which the money order fee of two annas had already been deducted. I would no longer find it difficult now to buy paper, nor would it be hard to get postage stamps for a while. My stories came out in many magazines such as *Keralapatrika* from Ernakulam, *Janashakthi* from Kochi and the *Madras Patrika*, which M. Govindan published from Madras.

I kept sending stories to *Jayakeralam* and *Mathrubhumi*; I sent one to K. Balakrishnan's *Kaumudi* as well. A letter written in English arrived, signed by Balakrishnan, saying, 'Your story moved me very much. I am publishing it soon.' The story appeared as he had promised in *Kaumudi* within two weeks. His magazine was no ordinary publication. A little later, a letter arrived and when I opened it, I found a cheque for ten rupees. A Travancore Forward Bank cheque. Someone else, not Balakrishnan, had signed the covering letter. To receive a cheque for ten rupees was an event, but I had to exchange it for money. None of my brothers were at home. Tatapuram Sukumaran had written an appreciative letter of encouragement to me when he came across some stories of mine in publications from Ernakulam and Kochi. I wrote to him saying I had received a cheque and asking how I could have it cashed. He replied at once, instructing me to write 'Contents received' on the back of the cheque, sign it and send it to him. He sent me a money order for nine rupees and odd within a week. I had other small debts to repay. Once, while going to Akkitham's place, I had stopped at Marar's hotel on the way and had tea and snacks, telling them I would pay on the way back. But unfortunately, Vasudevan had not been at home that day; it was from him that I used to occasionally borrow small sums. I avoided going to Marar's on two subsequent visits, aware of my debt. I had to repay some money I had borrowed to buy paper as well.

Jayakeralam was a publication with a high reputation. I sent them stories, but they were not accepted. However, they published two of my articles. *Chandrika* and *Kaumudi* had both paid me, so I thought *Jayakeralam* would too, but nothing arrived.

The following year, I joined Victoria College. All Achan could send was sixty rupees a month on a special permit. Hostel dues came up to about forty rupees and there were miscellaneous expenses. I was amazed to see how much money students who came from wealthy houses spent. I kept a discreet distance from them. The way they sauntered into hotels in the evenings to drink coffee, their outings to the cinema theatres on Saturdays: such things did not arouse my envy. But I watched the dhobi take freshly washed and ironed clothes into their rooms every week with a tinge of jealousy. I had brought only two shirts and two dhotis and they were all I had to get washed. There would be five or six shirts and as many double dhotis in the bundles brought back for others. I had to scrimp and save to keep back some money from what Achan sent, so that I would have enough to buy a ticket to go home for the vacation.

There were two short breaks every year before the summer vacation: Michaelmas and Christmas. A ticket from Olavakode to Pallippuram on a passenger train cost fourteen annas. If I had a rupee or two left after buying my ticket, I could manage to buy a paperback from the Higginbothams bookshop in Shoranur.

I applied for a BSc course, since someone had told me that it would be easy to get a job if I studied science.

But I realized that this was not true. Madras University announced that they were recruiting four or five chemistry demonstrators. I applied for the post and was called for an interview. The director of Collegiate Education was conducting the interview. At that period, there were colleges under the Madras University in Tamil Nadu as well as Andhra. I had no hope of securing the post. Some boys I had studied with were doing MA and MSc courses in Madras, and two of them were in Madras Christian College, Tambaram. They said I could stay with them.

Amma died during my final year of BSc. Only Cheriamma and her children now lived in Kudallur. Valiettan used to come home now and then. When I told him about the interview, he said, 'You don't have much chance of getting the job but go and try anyway.' The train fare from Shoranur to Madras in those days was six rupees. Radhakrishnan, who had been my classmate in Victoria College, came from Tambaram to meet me at the station in Madras. When the interview was over, I felt I would not get the job and went out with my old friends to see the city. A thought occurred to me suddenly: why not go to the *Jayakeralam* office? They had published several stories of mine and paid me for them as well, generally ten rupees for each story. They had published a long story once over two issues and paid me twelve rupees. Leaving my friends outside, I entered the *Jayakeralam* office (The Janatha Printing and Publishing Company) on Bells Road in Triplicane, full of the confidence that I was one of their writers. The editor, C.K. Appukutty Guptan, was not in. A bespectacled man was seated inside, reading proofs. I introduced myself and he asked me to sit down.

'Do you know how to read proofs?

'I can manage.'

He moved a few pages towards me, and I went through them. Then I told him why I had come. *Jayakeralam* had just started publishing books at the time. The first one they had printed was a novel by V.T. Nandakumar in installments. Following this, they had informed me that they were going to print a few of my stories as a collection. When the book came out (*Veyilum Nilavum,* Sunshine and Moonlight), they had sent me a copy. I told the gentleman very respectfully that I had come to Madras for an interview and that it would be a great help if he could give me some money towards royalties for my book.

His manner changed abruptly. He said angrily, surely I must have realized that they had done me a great favour in publishing my book. Money comes only when all copies are sold! I walked out, my eyes lowered and said nothing to my companions.

Many years later, Pai and Company opened a bookstall on Mount Road in Madras with the objective of creating a market for Malayalam books in the city. I was to inaugurate it. S.V. Pai had advertised the event well in *The Hindu.* He had also organized a dinner after the inauguration. I met the same *Jayakeralam* editor at the gathering. He was very effusive and while we talked, I mentioned the encounter I had had with him years earlier. Everyone was amused. But the editor-in-charge denied it hotly: 'This man is telling a whopping lie. Such a thing never happened!' S.V. Pai, V. Abdulla and others who were present had to rescue him from my furious attack, for I gripped him by the collar as he kept repeating that such an incident had never taken place!

Achan came back from Ceylon for good and settled down in Punnayurkulam. He had no savings at all but was able to survive because of the arable lands and coconut plantations he possessed, although he could not afford to indulge in any luxuries. Cheriamma, her children and Uncle Kuttan still lived in Kudallur. They had just enough to subsist on. Cheriamma found it difficult to manage our meals if any of us visited her since she would have to serve us some kind of snack in the mornings rather than the kanji they always had and then rice again for lunch instead of kanji. If it was a year when the mundaka, the second crop of the season had failed, paddy would be scarce. So, I would stay just a week in Kudallur and then go to Achan's place. If it happened to be a time when I had received a money order from *Jayakeralam,* I would stay for a couple of days in a room in Prabhakaran's lodge in Kunnamkulam. Prabhakaran, who was Uncle Madhavan's son, was my age. He had no interest in studies, so he had not finished his SSLC. There were a few engineering institutes in Kunnamkulam at that time that taught sundry courses and dispensed diplomas of some sort. Several students sought admission to these institutes merely to boast that they were doing an engineering course. Since Prabha was not short of money, he too enrolled in one of them, but he never talked about studies. We would roam around the bazaar, then watch a film in the theatre. Two days would go by like this, then I would go to Punnayurkulam.

There was an outer staircase in Achan's house that led to a veranda and his room was at one end of it. There was a swing-cot in his room. Achan was always careful to lock the room when he went out. After dinner at night, he would put on a shirt and walk down the lane, flashlight in hand.

Both Achan's sisters, Ammini oppu and Lakshmikutty oppu, grew suspicious about these outings. One of the women who came to work in the compound told them that he was going to see a woman in some tenement. One night, I followed the intermittently gleaming flashlight without letting his sisters know. I was quite frightened. What if Achan saw me, stopped and asked, where are you going? Once he had gone past the shops in Kunnathhoor, Achan turned left and went into a thatched cinema hall that had opened recently. Later, I heard him tell his friends who came to see him: 'When I lie down, I find I cannot sleep for a long time. So, I go and watch that bioscope in the theatre. One doesn't have to buy tickets for a show there, you know.' I imparted this piece of news to my aunts and the malicious gossip died down with that.

Achan did not ask me about my attempts at finding a job. Nor, if I stayed at his place for a period of five or six days, did he ever ask if I needed money to go back home. Once, when I arrived there, I learned that Uncle Madhavan would be visiting. They were busy cleaning the upstairs bedroom in the pathayappura for him. I don't quite know why, but everyone was nervous whenever Uncle Madhavan announced his visits. Most times, he would bring two or three suitcases along, but this time he brought only a small case. He was happy to see me. I used to write to him from college now and then and he would always reply. We wrote to each other in English. If Achan was there, he never came downstairs. They would smile at each other as soon as Uncle arrived and that was all. They ate their meals at different times. They were actually quite fond of one another, but Uncle Madhavan followed his own routine. He would walk up and down in the yard for a long time every evening. He always wore *kasavu*-bordered dhotis and thick gold chains around his neck. The fragrance of a spray he used enveloped him all the time.

This time, he had come to register the sale of a piece of land that he had bought, and Uncle Govindan was organizing the details of the transaction. Uncle Madhavan would go out into the yard a second time before dinner at night. At that point he would be quite intoxicated and would be shouting loudly at someone or other, even challenging some. No one knew who exactly he was raving at. No one had the guts to tell him to come in for dinner. Ammini oppu tried to encourage me to do so a couple of times, 'It's getting really late, ask him to come and eat, Vasu.' But I could never muster the courage to go anywhere near him.

Once the registration was over and Uncle was about to leave, all his sisters and nieces lined up on the veranda. As usual, he gave them all a severe look. I walked with him as he went down the lane. A taxi drew up, he smiled and climbed in. I hoped he would take out some money from his pocket and give it to me, but it did not happen.

After Uncle Madhavan left, I moved to his bedroom and spent my days on the veranda of the pathayappura. From time to time, Karthiyayani oppu would bring me some English books from the house of one of her classmates, most of which were crime novels.

Before leaving home, I had arranged for any money orders that came to be sent on to Punnayurkulam. I could not really hang around the post office there in the evening though, as I used to do in Kudallur. So, I waited, hoping the postman would turn up. I read three or four novels by Edgar Wallace. One evening, a few people from the neighbourhood came to see Achan. I saw water and glasses being taken to the veranda outside Achan's room. The voices from that side gradually grew louder, with Achan talking the most. I was beginning to feel hungry, but thought I would eat later, with Achan and his companions. They came to the dining room after a long time. A banana leaf had been laid for me, so I went and sat down. Achan lauded his sons' achievements as he ate. 'My eldest has a first class for his BA. He wrote an all-India exam and passed that as well. When the interview took place, he was dressed in khadi. Realizing that he sympathized with the national movement, they did not select him.' Achan did not seem upset about this. His son had gone to Madras, done an undergraduate course in teaching and become a teacher in a high school, which was a good thing. After all, Achan himself had started life as a teacher. The two younger boys were in the Railways. 'This youngest one hasn't yet found anything.' He was looking at me. 'Is he trying for something? We don't know that either. He had good marks for his BSc. But he's reading some book or other all the time. People say he scribbles things and sends them off to be published.' He went on and on in this strain. 'Even when it became difficult for me to send money from Ceylon, I used to send him expensive textbooks.' He had not sent that many, although it was true that he had sent me a textbook of inorganic chemistry by post and that it had been quite costly.

Achan's main accusation was that I was not attempting to find a job. I was very upset. I had just started to eat, but I got up quietly, went out, washed my hands and walked to the pathayappura.

Ammini oppu came looking for me after a while and said, 'Why did you come away without eating? Achan says all kinds of things, why should you take them to heart like this?' She tried hard to persuade me to go and eat, but I insisted I was done. I got up early next morning, brushed my teeth and had a bath. I had a clean shirt and dhoti in my bag. I changed into them, picked up my little bag and went downstairs. Ammini oppu was just about to climb the stairs to Achan's room, with tea in a brass lota and a bell-metal glass. 'Where are you going?' she asked.

'I have to go to Palakkad urgently.'

'I'll make you dosas quickly. Eat and go.'

'I have to leave at once.' Not waiting to explain any further, I walked out. In the lane, I looked at what I had in hand: a rupee and three annas. I walked on until I reached Kunnamkulam. I could go to Kudallur from there. The bus fare to Aaloor was eight annas. But I thought it best to go to Palakkad. Many boys I had studied with were there, I could stay with one of them for a few days. Some of them were looking for jobs, I would be able to check with them where to apply for one. But the bus fare from Kunnamkulam to Palakkad was two rupees.

I bought myself a tea and waited outside the little kiosk, gazing at the buses come and go, Suddenly, someone gave me a slap on my bottom. Startled, I turned around. A burning rope had been hung on the edge of the kiosk so that people who bought bidis or cigarettes could light them. I had been standing right next to it and the fire had burned a huge circle on the back of my shirt. The man who slapped me had put out the flame! My slightly better checked shirt! I moved aside. Some people at the bus stand kept calling out the destinations of each bus loudly and helped passengers get in. One of them, who had a handlebar moustache and a wad of betel leaves in his mouth, looked like their chief. I do not remember his name. Maybe because he had seen me there on several occasions, he looked at me as if he knew me. 'Where are you going, son?'

'To Palakkad.'

'The BBT will arrive at ten.'

He kept announcing the names of many places and helping people board. I hovered around him, then plucked up the courage to say, 'I'm not coming from home. I need two rupees.' He did not ask me any questions, expressed no doubts; just took out two rupees and asked, 'Is this enough?' Much later, when I had money of my own, I looked for him whenever I passed through Kunnamkulam so that I could repay my debt. But I never met him again. All that people who recognized him from my description could tell me was that he had left Kunnamkulam and was running a workshop with his son in Chalakudy or someplace like that.

None of the acquaintances I had assumed were in Palakkad were there. Finally, I found Aravindan, who always played a comedian's role in the plays produced by Appu Master for the college anniversary. Professor Appu had taught us drama and produced all our plays. I used to sometimes work behind the scenes, so I knew Aravindan and did not feel awkward about accepting his hospitality. I had published a few stories and had worked behind the scenes for some plays, so Aravindan thought it was fortunate that I had turned up to assist him. He had written a play that he wanted to stage on a grand scale in Palakkad town and I had arrived at an opportune moment.

Candidates who had not done their BT degree were being employed in high schools that were under the Malabar District Board in temporary posts. Aravindan suggested that I try for one of them. I could search for another job while I worked. I borrowed a small sum from him and went to Kudallur. Uncle Kuttan had come from Chalissery with the grievance that since the mahali disease had struck the areca palms, there were very few nuts to be plucked. Nevertheless, when I said to him, 'I have to go to Kozhikode to find a job', he gave me some money without showing any displeasure

It was my third trip to Kozhikode. My brother Kochunni ettan accompanied me. My brother Balettan had been working in a new magazine called *Dinaprabha* when I was studying for my SSLC examination and knew the writer Tikkodiyan, who worked there as well. The most important event during that trip was our meeting with Tikkodiyan. There was another Balettan in Kozhikode: our aunt Valiamma's son. He had a fairly high post at Pierce Leslie. We saw him rarely, but he was very fond of all of us. He was really pleased when we went to see him in his office. He instructed an attender to buy me lunch and asked me to go and see him before leaving the office. Balettan lived by himself in a small, rented house situated in a lane just off Jail Road. He had a cook. Balettan was not the sort who spoke much.

I broached the subject of my job to Balettan the following day. Pierce Leslie was a company owned by white men and it would not be easy for him to take me on as an employee there. I mentioned the high school job at that point. I could not stay on in Koodallur without a job of some kind. And anyway, I would not even get to see *The Hindu* newspaper which carried 'wanted' advertisements if I lived in Koodallur.

Balettan assured me that he would look into high school jobs. The superintendent of the District Board Office dealt with temporary posts and Balettan knew him well. He told me how to send an application and said I could stay in Kozhikode as long as I wanted. But I went back home and sent my application to the District Board from there.

A week later the appointment order arrived. For a vacancy lasting a few months in the Pattambi High School. As I packed my clothes and a few books in the suitcase I had used at the time I was in college, I thought to myself: with my salary of sixty-nine rupees, I can put aside a little money after my expenses and buy some clothes. A new shirt every month and a new dhoti. One or two pairs of pants if possible . . .

Pattambi was close by but was not a place I knew much about. I left my suitcase in a little shop and went to the school. A small surprise awaited me: S.R. Subramania Ayyar, who had been the headmaster of Kumaranallur High School where I had done my SSLC, was the headmaster here! He knew my elder brother, M.T. Govindan Nair, who was a teacher and he remembered me as a bright student in his class in Kumaranallur. He signed some papers and said, 'This vacancy exists because Keshavan Namboodiri has gone on leave. I don't know if he will extend his leave. As of now, this post will last about six months.' The subject he taught was composite mathematics and it would be difficult to change the timetable. So, I would have to teach his classes. Subramania Ayyar emphasized this since he had noted on my certificate that the subjects I had studied for my BSc were chemistry, botany and zoology. I agreed. In the staff room, I met a comparatively young teacher, Ramakrishnan from Kozhikode. He had done mathematics for his BSc and was willing to help me.

That evening, the Malayala Samajam was being inaugurated. Ullattil Govindankutty Nair was the chief guest and P.G. Pattambi another guest. We received news that Govindankutty Nair had to take to bed because of a fever. The chief teacher of Malayalam, Ravi Namboodiripad, knew my eldest brother, Valiettan. He said that apart from P.G. Pattambi, someone else had to give a speech, otherwise the meeting would become uninteresting. At this point, one of the teachers asked me, 'Master, don't you write stories?' I answered shyly, 'Yes.' Another person suggested, 'Then we could ask this master to speak, couldn't we?'

The teacher from Kozhikode asked, 'What about it, Master?'

I had often made speeches in college and had not found it a difficult task. So, I accepted, reminding myself that I was now a 'Master' in school. I took care to deliver a fairly good speech at the meeting, not because it seemed necessary, but because I wanted the students to think their new teacher was a talented person.

There was a building with six rooms next to a *kovilakam*, which had once been the residence of a branch of a royal family, situated on the river's bank. All were single rooms and I managed to get one which had fallen vacant. Apart from Ramakrishnan, there were two other teachers, Rama Varier and Ramankutty Varier and two teachers of physical education, Francis and Uthupuru, as well.

That night, we all met one another. Ramankutty Varier asked very hopefully, 'Master, do you play cards?'

'A bit,' I answered.

'Do you play fifty-six?'

'I don't really know how to play it well.'

'We play fifty-six here every night.'

They were short of a player. The clerk in the railways who used to come and play with them had been transferred. Francis and Uthupuru had no interest in playing cards. Most nights, I had to prepare for the next day's class in composite mathematics, so I stayed away from card-playing.

The two Variers had arranged for a boy to bring tea and breakfast from a hotel at about seven every morning and they had ordered it for me as well. Usually, the hotel sent an aappam wrapped in a banana leaf. This was not enough for me at all and what really astonished me was the way the Variers ate it. There was no gravy of any sort with the aappam, just a little sugar. They would spend a long time eating it bit by bit and when they finished the last morsel, they would run their fingers over the grains of sugar left on the leaf and end their morning meal by licking them clean. I gradually realized that not ordering more than one aappam was their way of controlling their expenses. I was reluctant to order more than one while they contented themselves with a single aappam. A few days later, Ramankutty Varier suggested a change: a tea as soon as we got up and no aappams at all. Around eight thirty or eight-thirty-five, we could go and have a meal at Bharatha Ayyar's hotel, where lunch would be ready by that time. If we ate a full meal and went to school, we could avoid spending money on lunch at noon. Around three o'clock, a boy always brought a glass of tea to the teachers' room. We could have a full meal again at night in Bharatha Ayyar's hotel.

Ramakrishnan used to have lunch in another hotel near the spot where one came out from the station. It was a little costlier than the meal at Bharatha Ayyar's. I decided to accompany him there. I had been perspiring profusely after eating hot rice at eight thirty every morning. I realized that the Varier Masters, who had families and children, were trying hard to send as much money home as they could spare from their meagre budgets. They did not have the freedom that I, single as I was, enjoyed on my salary of sixty-nine rupees. Looking at them, I did not have the heart to order two aappams for myself for breakfast. So, I began to go with Ramakrishnan to a small shop nearby for breakfast. At that period, most of the talk in the teachers' room centred on a possible increase in the salary scale. Later, whenever I remembered that phase of my life, a picture of the Varier Masters eating their aappam would take shape in my mind.

My appointment was going to end after five months, for Keshavan Namboodiri was coming back. I was transferred to Chavakkad High School, maybe for three or four months. Teachers who had worked in many places told me that Sadashivayyar, the headmaster of the Chavakkad School, was a frightful person. I did go there and start working, but it did not last more than a week. The headmaster scolded me for some minor reason and I walked out without saying anything to him. I had been sharing a small house with the music master. As I picked up my little suitcase and stepped out, I asked myself: where to now?

Valiaettan was teaching in the Kumaranallur High School at the time and staying in Balan Nair's rented house, the same house we had lived in as children. There was a newly built bathroom now outside. I did not tell my brother that I had left after a quarrel with the headmaster. Preparations were under way for the silver jubilee in his school. I began to participate in them enthusiastically. The play being presented was Tikkodiyan's *Jeevitham* (Life).

The poet Akkitham's younger brother was playing the role of the teacher who was the heroine. A shadow play would be performed afterwards. The poets G. Sankara Kurup and Olappamanna had been invited. I was sent to bring Kurup Master from the railway station in a taxi. While waiting for the train to arrive, I picked up the *Mathrubhumi* newspaper from the little bookstall there and read a news item: I had been awarded the prize for the Malayalam story in the World Short Story Competition, a story called 'Valarthumrigangal' (Pet Animals). Kurup Master congratulated me during the seminar. I have written about this incident elsewhere.

I had no idea when I would receive my prize. Therefore, I still had to find a job. I heard that the poet Akkitham had come home, so I went to see him. He told me that he had written a letter from Thrissur, congratulating me on getting the prize, but I had not received it. It had been sent to my Koodallur address and was probably lying somewhere in the house. When I spoke to Akkitham about feeling distressed at not having a job, he said, 'Go to M.B. Tutorial in Palakkad if you like. They are thinking of starting a weekly or a magazine. Though it is only a tutorial, it is a big institution. They need people to teach there as well.' He gave me a letter of introduction to C.K. Moosad. So, I set out once again to Palakkad with my old steel case.

Krishnan Moosad ran the office. Although C.K. Moosad was the principal, I realized that Krishnan Moosad, the middle brother, was the administrator. He read Akkitham's letter and said with real pleasure, 'I cannot offer you a huge salary. But you can certainly stay here, Vasudevan Nair.'

I was allowed to stay in one of the classrooms and the others there shared the food that was brought to them with me. I taught natural science, but sometimes had to teach Malayalam as well. Being a tutorial, there was no strict timetable. If no teacher was available for a class, I had to step in and handle it.

I enjoyed all of it. Krishnan Moosad gave me my salary at the end of the month, mentioning that they had settled on the sum of sixty rupees. Holding back the twenty-five rupees I owed for food, he gave me the remaining thirty-five rupees. I was content. I had a room to sleep in and food. I could live well on the money left over. The tutorial would close after the exams in March and until June, students who had failed their exams would join. There was no salary during the vacation. We had to write guides during that period. I wrote guides for chemistry, botany and zoology. Balaraman Moosad's name and mine were printed on a guide for the SSLC Malayalam syllabus. I enjoyed my two years in the tutorial. I wrote stories from time to time, *Jayakeralam* published most of them.

There was no function when the *Mathrubhumi* Prize was awarded. My story appeared in a weekly issue, together with a short article I had written on the circumstances in which I wrote it. A cheque arrived with the prize money of five hundred rupees. Since the Moosad brothers dealt regularly with a bank, they cashed the cheque and gave me the money. It was a huge sum for me, and I thought I should not spend it. I had heard that Achan's situation in Punnayurkulam had grown much worse. I went there, spent a day and gave him the money as I was leaving. I told him it was the prize money I had received for writing a story. I left hastily, not bothering to note how he responded. I could have kept a hundred for myself and given him four hundred, but somehow, I wanted to give him the whole sum. I had already looked through advertisements and sent applications to many places for jobs.

I was staying in the deserted tutorial by myself during the vacation. Thangappan, the peon, brought me my meals and tea from a small hotel on College Road. One day, when he brought me tea, he said that the owner of the tea shop had told him rather seriously that the sum of money I owed him for my food was steadily increasing. I was aware of this: I had not paid for my tea or meals for over a month. Who could I write to for some cash? Although all my older brothers were working, none of them earned big salaries. When lunchtime came around, Thangappan hung around uneasily, tiffin carrier in hand. I asked him to wait. I had enough money with me for a tea and lunch. What would the hotel owner think if he caught sight of Thangappan with a tiffin carrier? This fellow has started buying on credit in another place without paying what he owes me!

I saw a car stop at the gate. Three people got out. Maybe they had not realized the tutorial was closed and had come to meet the Moosads. I stood up as they came in. There were some chairs on the veranda, I asked them to sit down.

'The Moosad Masters have gone to their village,' I said.

One of the visitors asked, 'Aren't you Vasudevan Nair?'

'Yes.'

'I've seen your photograph in *Jayakeralam*.'

He and his companions had come from Thiruvananthapuram. His name was George Netto and he was from Singapore. He was going to start a publishing house in Thiruvananthapuram. They were getting some books ready for publication, one of them being a collection of my stories. They had already selected the stories they would include. And they had chosen a title as well: 'Olavum Theeravum'.

I accepted. I was happy. I had been thinking of approaching the well-known Mangalodayam Press, which enjoyed a great reputation then, to ask if they would publish a collection of my stories, a task that was not easy at all. And here was a publisher ready to do so! I would have liked to welcome them with tea, but there was no way I could manage that. Netto and his companions were leaving at once, they had to get to an estate in Mannarghat. We would engage via correspondence about the short story collection. Netto started to say goodbye. He took out an envelope from his pocket, and smiling, said: 'This is towards your royalties. We'll settle the accounts later, after the book comes out.'

He gave it to me and went out. I opened the envelope once their car had moved away from the gate into the distance.

Notes! Brand new five-rupee notes! I counted them— two hundred rupees. It reminded me of the legend about my house: when a widow and her children who lived there were starving, Bhagavathi, the Mother Goddess of the Kodikunnath temple, brought them a potful of cooked rice at midnight. It must surely be the blessing of that Mother Goddess that had brought George Netto here.

I called Thangappan and asked him to settle the dues at Nair's hotel and bring me my lunch and half a packet of Berkeley cigarettes. In the evening, I walked to the New Theatre and watched a Hindi film. On my way back I had chappathis and mutton curry at Madras Café. I should not throw away money because I had a huge sum in hand, I reminded myself. Next day, I went to Kozhikode.

Valiamma's son Balettan was not there—he had gone to
Coimbatore for a week on some work. I took a room in
Modern Hotel. The Radha Theatre was right opposite and
Thikurussi's *Shariyo Thetto* (Right or Wrong) was playing
there. I bought a ticket for the second show. The next day,
I boarded a train to Pallippuram. Then to Kudallur, where
I spent a night. Then back to Palakkad. Cheriamma was
distressed that I was going back without staying a few days
in Kudallur. Vilasini, her daughter, gave me two letters that
had come for me. I wrote down my Palakkad address for
her and told her that if the postman brought letters for me
anytime, she must ask him to redirect them to the address:
Lecturer, M.B.T. College, College Road, Palakkad. If I said,
tutorial college, what if people thought it was a trivial job?
When I sent off stories in my college days, I used to give the
address, G.V.C. Nandakumar, College Road, Palakkad.
G.V.C. Nandakumar was the name of the hostel located
at the gate of our college. If I wrote 'hostel', what if they
thought I was only a student? So, I tweaked the address.
My name in the college register was M.T. Vasudevan. I
added Nair so that when someone in a newspaper office
opened an envelope I had sent, they would presume I was
a grown man.

One of the letters I had received at home was about
a job I had applied for some time earlier. The post was
that of a rural development assistant or something
like that. When the advertisement came out, they had
mentioned details: degree holders would be appointed as
grade-one assistants and those who had passed the SSLC
Examination would be grade-two assistants. I had written
a qualifying examination as well, conducted in the V.V.P.
School in Palakkad. I had almost forgotten about all this.

The letter said that training would begin for the selected candidates the following week at the agricultural farm in Thaliparambu. There would be a stipend of sixty-five rupees throughout the training period. A list of things the trainees had to bring with them was included: two sets of khadi shirts and trousers, a broom, a bucket, pots and pans, glasses and all sorts of other articles.

I went to Palakkad and made ready for the journey. I wrote to Valiettan, giving him the information. He replied at once. It was a good move: a government job. A huge department dedicated to block development was going to be created. Aravindan's cousin Sridharan had received a similar letter and was considering it seriously. Our accommodation would be on the Gandhian model. When the training was over, the degree holders would be appointed block development officers. Sridharan had found out that it was a good post. He had already bought khadi clothes. Sridharan assured me that I could buy a bucket, a broom and things like that in Payyanoor, near Thaliparambu.

'Let me go and see. Gandhian training is okay. But if we have to clean out the latrines, I'll come back.'

I wrote a letter to Krishnan Moosad, gave it to Thangappan and boarded a train to Kannur with Sridharan. We would go on to Thaliparambu from there.

It was a very large farm. The hostel was comfortable. The office peon showed us our single rooms. Officially, training would begin the following day. That evening, there was to be a meeting for all the trainees and the director would speak to us.

We gathered in the hall. There were some others from Palakkad. The director would welcome us and then give a speech. An officer would explain the details of the training programme to us, and one of us representing the trainees had to give a vote of thanks. Maybe because the Palakkad group suggested it, this responsibility fell to me. Sridharan and the others came to my room after lunch. Many of them had doubts about Gandhian principles of training and that was what we talked about. Suddenly, the director appeared at the door. I was smoking a cigarette.

Without entering the room, he pointed a finger at me and said, 'Smoking is not allowed.'

'Sorry, Sir.' I stubbed out the cigarette. He stared at me for a while and left.

Everyone fell silent and went back to their rooms. The next morning, we were all supposed to be present at a certain spot at eight-thirty, but I had not seen the notice saying this posted in the hostel. I got up, bathed, got ready and went to the canteen for breakfast only to find that none of my companions were there. They had gone to the ground. Where was this ground? I ran as fast as I could and reached a place full of people.

Once I realized that all these people were in grade two, I began running again, trying to find the spot where grade one was. The director and a teacher were speaking to the grade-one trainees, who numbered around thirty. I pushed my way to the front and the director glanced at his watch and signed to me to stand aside. I moved away quietly. They were talking about the things we had to buy on our way back. When I returned to my room, a peon came and said that the director had asked me to go to his office. My companions watched me go. One of them said, 'Probably, you've been summoned because you were two minutes late this morning.'

The director was looking at some papers in the office. He must have seen me enter, but he raised his eyes only after quite some time.

Then he began to speak. 'You know you are a government servant.'

He said many other things about the responsibilities that a government job entailed and the discipline. His English was good. At some point, he stopped speaking and gave me a *look*. 'You understand?'

'Yes, Sir.'

'Now get out.'

As I was walking out of the door I turned around and said, 'I am getting out not only from your office but also from this place.'

I got back to my room and started to pack. Two of the members of my group came in to find out what had happened.

'Nothing,' I said. 'I'm leaving. One of you please come with me up to the road.'

A bus bound for Kannur arrived at once. My friends lifted my suitcase on to the bus. I did not feel upset at all as I left. Nor did I worry that I had thrown away the government job I had got. My older brothers would not ask me why I had left.

Kannur was another town that I did not know well. I remembered the name of a hotel that a boy from Kannur had mentioned in our college days. I gave a coolie my case and said, 'Madhava Nivas.'

The hotel was an old house to which minor renovations had been made. At night, I went for a short walk along the seashore. As I was about to go to bed I remembered: Thangam from Punnayoor was studying in Kannur at the

Teachers' Training College. She was Uncle Madhavan's aunt's elder sister's daughter, the same age as I was. I went in search of the training school in the morning and learnt that Thangam had fallen ill and been in bed for almost ten days in the hostel. I had to wait a long time in the hostel before she came out. She had grown very weak, become miserably thin and changed so much, I could hardly recognize her. The moment she saw me, she began to cry. She had been running a high fever. The hostel warden had arranged for a doctor to come and see her. He said he thought it might be typhoid. She had to have three injections and medicines as well. There had been no reply to the letter she wrote home. She kept crying and did not ask how I had found my way there.

'All I want is to somehow get home. I do not have a single paisa. The doctor said the fever would go up if I don't have injections. I need money for that, don't I?'

I was busy making calculations in my mind. I would not have to pay more than eight or ten rupees to Madhava Nivas. I knew without having to count that what remained in my pocket of the new notes that Netto had given me would add up to seventy rupees. I took fifty rupees out, put back ten and gave forty rupees to Thangam, saying, 'I have some money. Take those injections. And then go home if you want to. There's enough here for all that.'

She took the money, wiped her tears and gazed at the floor.

'I'm going, Thangam.'

'Your job now?'

'I have one. In Palakkad. I don't have any problems.'

I walked out. I entered a telegraph office and sent Krishnan Moosad a telegram: 'I will be coming back to Palakkad tomorrow to work again in the tutorial.'

Then I walked on to Madhava Nivas with a great sense of relief.

Glossary

aandiyoottu	a meal for the pilgrims going to Pazhani
ada prathaman	a sweet made with mashed fruit or lentils, cooked in coconut milk and jaggery
Amarakosham	a Sanskrit dictionary
anna	a former monetary unit of India and Pakistan, equal to one sixteenth of a rupee
athol	derived from *akathe aval*, 'she who lives inside', added to the name of a Namboodiri woman
Bhagavathi	the Mother Goddess
Bharathapuzha	a river in central Kerala, also known as the Nila
bull festival	a festival at which people dance, carrying dummy bulls made of straw
chavattila-poothan	for this poothan, the costumes are made of dried coconut fronds

Cheriambra	a variation of 'Cheria' (meaning 'little')
Chettichi, Chetty	a caste originally from Tamil Nadu, settled in Kerala
chinnan	the last breath drawn at the time of death
dakshina	donation
dhara	anointing with oil, milk, etc.
elassu	a metal locket with a talisman inside
Elayad	a caste associated with funeral rites
Embralma	a form of address used by lower castes for women of a higher caste
Embrandiri	a Brahmin, originally from Karnataka, settled in Kerala
Ezhuthacchan	a caste, many members of which are teachers
forms	the child starts in Class 1. There are four classes. Class 5 is the First Form. There are six forms. This was the system in all schools.
gulikan	evil planet
illam	the residence of a Namboodiri
inangan	a distant relative of the family who takes part in all rituals
kalasham	a purification ceremony
kalathekku	a contraption operated by bulls to water the field
kappu	a thick bangle

karimkali	a dancer who performs at a temple festival wearing a Kali costume
karyasthan	a steward or manager of a large estate
kasavu	the gold border that edges the off-white cotton saris and dhotis woven in Kerala
kashu	a coin that was used in Kerala in olden times
kathirkkola	a bell-shaped sheaf of paddy grains hung upside down
kavathu kizhangu	a kind of tuber
Kavu	a temple dedicated to Bhagavathi, the Mother Goddess
kindi	a vessel made of bell-metal or copper, with a spout
kirtanam	a devotional song
konakam	a long piece of material used to cover the genitals, made from cloth or from a tender palm spathe
koothu	a performance conducted in a temple during which the artiste dances and narrates a story
koothumadam	the area where a koothu is performed
kovilakam	principal manor or estate of a princely lineage of Kerala
kurma	a South Asian dish or sauce made with cream or yogurt, and often almonds
kuruthi	a sacrificial puja for Bhagavathi

machu	attic
mahali	a disease that strikes areca-nut palms
Mamangam	a festival that was in vogue in medieval Kerala, celebrated once in twelve years
Moosad	a caste that serves in temples
mathokku	tapioca
mundaka	this season starts in September and continues till January
nadappura	corridor
nadaswaram	traditional music played at south Indian Hindu weddings
nalukettu	a house built around a rectangular courtyard open to the sky; the word also refers to the courtyard itself
navara kizhi	poultices used in massage treatment
nazhi	smallest unit of measure of rice and paddy
Onam	a festival celebrated over ten days in August–September
oordhvan	the last breath drawn at the time of death
paalkavadi	an offering made to Lord Muruga
paathi	a flat wooden receptacle
padmam	a lotus-shaped design
padippura	the gatehouse
pagida	the dice used in a game
pana-poothan	poothan who belongs to the Panar community

para	a measure of paddy or rice, approximately 12 kilograms
para-poothan	poothan who belongs to the Paraya community
pathayappura	an outhouse
payasam	a sweet made with rice, milk and sugar
poothans	dancers wearing different types of masks who come to houses during temple festivals
prasadam	food, flowers and sandal paste offered to the deity and then distributed to devotees
prasnam	a ritual conducted to find out what evil influences have provoked misfortune
punja	this season starts in December–January and goes on till April
puttu	a snack usually made with rice flour. Here, it is made with powdered bamboo grain
puzhukku	a dish made of boiled/steamed root vegetables, flavoured with seasoned coconut paste
rajavembala	a king cobra
serpent shrine	serpent worship was very popular in Kerala. Most households had a small shrine dedicated to serpent gods within their compound. Daily rituals and worship in these shrines were compulsory.

serpent thullal	snake dance. A traditional ritual performed annually in Kerala's joint family households to appease the snake gods.
sindooram	vermilion
sudarshanam	Vishnu's wheel
thalapoli	a procession of women carrying platters decorated with lighted oil lamps and auspicious objects
Thamburan	a respectful way of addressing a person of a higher social status; was used by people who belonged to the so-called inferior castes to address people of higher castes. Thamburan, masculine, Thamburatti, feminine
tharam	arrack
tharavad	the extended Namboodiri/Nair household; in the case of Nairs, of matrilineal descent
thecchi	a flowering plant. The flowers are used for pujas.
thekkini	a room on the southern side of the house
thira	dancers wearing semicircular discs of carved wood as headgear
umikkari	burnt husk of paddy used for cleaning teeth
uruli	a flat metal dish
vadikkini	a room on the northern side of the house adjacent to the kitchen, used freely by women

vaidyan	physician/medicine-man
vela	a temple festival
vibhuti	sacred ash
Vishu	the Malayalam New Year, the first day of the month of Medam
Virippu	first season of cultivation, the first crop. Mundaka is the second crop and punja the third

Scan QR code to access the
Penguin Random House India website